READY

steady

GLOW

READY

steady

GLOW

Fresh, fast food designed for real life

MADELEINE SHAW

contents

introduction

This book was written to make healthy eating a breeze, to do away with the myth that nourishing your body takes time and work. With *Ready, Steady, Glow* you can live healthily, on the go. You'll find cooking my recipes quicker than ordering a pizza!

I understand that life is a balancing act. Like a lot of you, I work long hours during the week and get home late in the evening. I don't want to slave away at the hob for hours. All I want is a quick, easy and tasty meal before I slip into my pyjamas and head to bed!

But when the weekend comes, I cherish those two precious days. It's my opportunity to focus on me, to relax, to catch up with loved ones and to indulge in food that I don't have time to make during the week. That's why I have written *Ready, Steady, Glow*; it's a book of two halves – Fast Weeks and Slow Weekends – a book that reflects how we eat now.

I received such wonderful feedback from my first book, *Get the Glow*, and it makes my heart sing that you all enjoy cooking my food. Many of you reported that being time-poor during the week got in the way of eating healthily, so I'm here to help. In Part

One: Fast, all the recipes can be made in less than 30 minutes, so there is no excuse for ordering a takeaway or picking up a ready-meal on the way home! To make your life even easier, in this section you'll notice that all the recipes feature a clock in the margin that denotes exactly how long it takes to make each one, so you really can eat healthily in a matter of minutes.

In Part Two: Slow, you'll find recipes that are still easy to make but require a little more time to cook. You can indulge yourself with a slow roast or lazy brunch, and de-stress while you bake a delicious cake. This is also your opportunity to prep for the week ahead, giving you the best chance of keeping on the right track on busy days. You'll also find tips on how to eat healthily while out and about, how to motivate yourself to stay on this path and how to banish overeating. I've also included my 15-minute full-body yoga routine to set you up for the day ahead.

As ever, all my recipes are sugar- and wheat-free, this being the way I transformed my own body and health. I was 18 and living in Australia when I developed painful IBS. I sought the help of specialists and doctors, but it was while working in a health-food café on Bondi Beach that I discovered the transformational power of eating wholesome, proper foods. My IBS disappeared, my energy levels skyrocketed and my skin started to glow.

It was then that I decided to dedicate my life to health and nutrition, and to spreading the wellness word. I studied at the Institute for Integrative Nutrition, began writing a

blog and started to work with others on overhauling their health and bodies.

I'm often asked if my programme results in weight loss. The answer is 'Yes', you will see results. But I'm not interested in being a weight-loss guru, and neither do I advocate counting calories. I want you to love food, and to love your body. I want to make healthy living simple and easy so you can make it a way of life. So Ready... Steady... Glow! Let's go...

Madeleine

how to use this book

Ready, Steady, Glow is a cookbook designed for real life. It reflects how we eat now; it caters for our busy schedules as well those precious moments when we have the luxury of enough time to spend making something really indulgent. And, above all, every recipe is simple, easy to put together and full of wholesome ingredients that will nourish your beautiful body.

The recipes that follow are divided into two sections: fast and slow. The 'fast' recipes can be made in less than 30 minutes, meaning they're perfect for the busy weekdays when all you want is a wholesome dinner on the table, pronto, so you can curl up on the sofa to watch your favourite box set. Of course, life shouldn't just be about speed; we need to take care of ourselves and make time to relax, destress and unwind in among the rushing around. That's what the weekends are for, and there's no better way to slow down than by hitting your local shops or farmers' market, choosing which ingredients to buy, and savouring food that takes a little longer to prepare. These are the recipes contained in the 'slow' section of this book. This is food that can be enjoyed on your own or with friends and family. But this doesn't mean these recipes are complicated – they are still easy to prepare and contain ingredients you can find in your local supermarket.

I know that the pressures and stresses of everyday life can get in the way of maintaining a healthy lifestyle. I don't believe in quick-fix diets – they're always doomed to fail – but a bit of preparation and some simple shortcuts can go a long way to keeping you on the right track. Here's my advice on how to plan your week ahead.

saturday

Saturday mornings are my 'me time'; having spent so much of my week rushing around for work and catching up with other people, I make sure that nothing and no one intrudes on these precious few hours at the weekend.

First up, I run through my 15-minute yoga routine (see pages 252–67) – it's such a great way to get the weekend off on the right track. Then I grab a notebook, make a basic plan of the meals I want to make for the week ahead (see my meal plans on pages 246–51 and remember to double up the quantities so you can batch cook) and check my cupboards for supplies. I urge you to do the same – make a list of what you're missing from my essential ingredients listed on pages 17–27, along with the fresh produce you'll need to prep your meals for the week ahead (but remember to multiply the quantities if you are planning to batch-cook any dishes!).

List in hand, I hop on my bike and head for my local farmers' market. It's great to meet the producers, sample food that is grown locally and buy fresh ingredients that I can rely on. I know that shopping this way can be more expensive than going to the supermarket, but if you plan well you'll find you have less waste and therefore more money to spare. How many times have you been lured in by a multi-buy offer, only to have that courgette languish until it's limp at the bottom of the fridge but you didn't get round to using it?

Most Saturday afternoons I do absolutely nothing. And I mean *nothing*. It's total bliss. Ask yourself, when was the last time you took time to rest? To curl up on the sofa, read, or lie in bed? If the answer is yesterday, good on ya, but most of us fill every waking hour with an activity, lunch date, housework . . . Busy has become the social norm.

So I want you to take back your weekend and give yourself at least an hour of rest. This doesn't mean a walk or anything active; it means an hour to chill. I love to grab a notebook and scribble down my thoughts or draw. It doesn't matter what you do, it just needs to feel calming. Often we feel uneasy about being still; we grab our phones, or check our emails or social media. Learning to be mindful is the best way to banish stress – so make time to do this just as you would an important meeting.

On a Saturday night I tend to either head to a dinner at a friend's house or host one myself. Getting asked over for a dinner party is wonderful – I get to eat delicious food without having to do the washing up! But when I began this wellness journey, being invited out to eat did make me worry about undoing all the good work I'd put in. I'm pretty lucky now that most people try to cook healthily when I come over, but early on I just had to be honest and explain what I was trying to achieve with my food choices. My advice is to give your friends a little warning beforehand, or perhaps offer to take a dish with you. Remember, if you don't ask, you don't get: if they're true friends they'll support what you're doing.

I know that it isn't always possible to influence what someone else cooks for you, and it's probably not the best approach when you meet the in-laws for the first time! In this situation you've just got to relax: one naughty meal won't hurt. Instead of feeling guilty, why not take inspiration from what you've been served and try to recreate a 'clean' version of it at home later?

If you're hosting, you're sorted. Here's my favourite dinner party menu, which always goes down a treat:

Starter: Life-Changing Spicy Tomato Soup (pages 74–5) served in a small glass with fresh coriander

Main: Whole Apricot-Glazed Chicken (pages 196–7) with Roast Pumpkin, Shaved Fennel and Watercress Salad (pages 194–5)

Dessert: Raw Toffee Chocolate Sticks (pages 240–1) and Baked Strawberry and Raspberry Tart (pages 226–7)

You can make this soup in the morning and keep it chilled in the fridge until you want to serve it. Don't forget, any leftover roast chicken makes a great protein to add to salads for the week ahead.

sunday

Sunday is a great day to prep and batch-cook for the coming week. Choose what you're going to make and double up the quantities so you have batches ready for a future date. Life suddenly becomes a lot easier when you have a stocked fridge and ready-made meals. Most food will last 3–4 days in the fridge, so unless you're planning to freeze what you prepare, don't cook for beyond that. You can do some batch-cooking mid-week, too, if you need to top up your supplies.

I suggest that you look to the busy week ahead and target your trouble times: if you start work early and never have time for breakfast, whip up my overnight oats on pages 70–1 (which last three days in the fridge) so you can walk out of the door with a Tupperware full, ready to eat when you get to your desk. Or if you work late, make a big pot of soup to heat up when you get home. My Red Thai Sweet Potato and Lentil Soup (pages 80–1) is one of my favourite weekend wonders: I keep a bowl saved for lunch in the week, when I team it with rye bread or my Spinach Bread (pages 180–1). Stews like my Chicken and Olive Tagine (pages 134–5) or Moroccan Spiced Stew (pages 202–3) are also great to prep on a

Sunday to warm up after a long day at work.

I also tend to make some salads to pack into lunch boxes, like my Mango and Avocado Salad (pages 96–7) or my Beauty Buddha Bowl (pages 112–3). Again, both last a few days in the fridge and work well as side dishes to a main meal in the evening.

Of course, you don't have to prep entire meals if you don't want to: you could cook some quinoa, cut up some veggie crudités, roast a pumpkin and boil a couple of eggs so that you have some snacks in the fridge to grab and go. I always tend to have a batch of Raw Mango and Coconut Bites (pages 104–5) on-hand to keep the sugar monster at bay!

monday – thursday

By now you should have a clear idea of what you're planning to cook for your evening meals ahead. My philosophy is to cook once, eat twice – so remember to always factor in an extra portion to take to work with you for tomorrow's lunch. Lots of recipes taste even better when warmed up the next day, such as my Chickpea Curry or Sweet Potato Noodle Salad (pages 118–9 and 86–7). Just throw in a handful of extra green goodness, such as spinach, rocket or watercress to give it a boost.

I'm huge fan of converting leftovers into lunchbox treats. Any leftover Apricot-Glazed Chicken (pages 196–7) from your Sunday feast can be chucked into a box with half an avocado, a baby gem lettuce and lemon and olive oil dressing. I often pop my Bloat-Free BLT (pages 152–3) into a Tupperware in my handbag and enjoy it sitting on a park bench, if the weather is nice.

If you forget your lunch or don't have enough time to prep, don't worry! Rather than buy a sandwich, head down to your local supermarket, grab some protein (e.g. smoked salmon/mackerel, cooked chicken, boiled eggs or cooked quinoa, etc.), add in some veg (an avocado, tomato, grated carrot or cooked beetroot) and a handful of green leaves (rocket, spinach, watercress, lettuce), top it with some crunch (e.g. nuts or seeds) and drizzle over a lovely dressing. A bottle of olive oil, some mustard and sea salt is easy to store in your drawer at work, with a little jar to mix it up so you can make the perfect dressing every time.

Top tip: Never dress your salad in the morning before you go to work as it'll go soggy. Instead, use an old spice jar to carry your dressing in separately.

friday

Ah, there's nothing better than that Friday feeling! The weekend is here, and if you're like me you'll either feel ready to P-A-R-T-Y or you'll be craving your sofa, a film and a takeaway. But eating out and takeaways can be tricky to navigate on your journey to glowing health.

If you're eating out, my advice is to never feel embarrassed to choose the healthy option. I spent years feeling awkward when ordering a salad rather than a burger like my friends. Why? Because I made them feel guilty. Remember why you eat healthily: to fuel YOUR beautiful body. Don't worry about what others think; they're whining because they feel bad about their food choices.

It's amazing how the world of healthy eating has changed, with most restaurants offering gluten-free options, grass-fed meat and delicious, wholesome salads. Just because you're in an Italian restaurant, it doesn't mean you have to order pizza! Look for the options that are made up of a clean protein and veggies. At a Thai restaurant you could order a Thai beef salad or a vegetable stir-fry; just remember to ask for no sauce as it always contains added sugar. If pub grub is your bag, the steak or fish of the day is a good choice, accompanied by a side of fresh veggies. Just say no to the bread basket and ask to swap chips for salad.

I love takeaways as much as the next person – you can't beat the convenience – but I don't think we'll be seeing kale and quinoa on the menus any time soon! You can still make healthy choices, though, such as opting for dishes that mainly comprise protein and veg: e.g. rotisserie chicken and salad. If Indian food is your thing, order a tandoori meat platter, or kebabs – dishes that aren't covered in greasy or creamy sauces – and order a side salad to go with it rather than rice and bread.

I know not every takeaway menu has a 'clean' option, but choose sensibly and as long as it's a treat and not a weekly occurrence, just enjoy it!

my food philosophy

Food is my first passion and is at the heart of this book. I'm not Paleo, vegetarian or vegan; I prescribe a more flexible approach to healthy living and I follow these nine golden rules:

1. **Hydrate:** I know water isn't food but it's the best thing to hit your lovely lips in the morning. Think hydrate before you caffeinate. Aim to drink two large glasses of warm water with freshly grated ginger upon rising. Then throughout the day drink 3.3 per cent of your body weight in water. Try to consume clean filtered water to remove unwanted chemicals, bacteria and pathogens. Proper hydration gives you boundless energy and glowing skin.

2. **Up ya protein:** Some adverts have led us to believe that cereal is the best way to start the day, but really we are pumping our bodies with buckets of sugar and chemicals that leave us groggy and reaching for coffee and cake at 11 a.m. Switching to a protein-powered breakfast will fuel you until lunchtime: no slumps, no snacks. Don't skip this one: it really works. You can also up ya protein through grass-fed meat, fish, eggs, quinoa, nuts, seeds, beans and legumes.

3. **Don't diet or deprive:** This isn't a diet, it's a lifestyle. Telling yourself you can't have something makes you want it more. It's like being a kid again! It's time to master your mindset. Start looking at food as something that nourishes your body, that boosts your energy, makes your skin shine bright and is always a pleasure to eat. Focus on crowding in, not cutting out. You will be filling your plate with lots of delicious veggies, fresh fruits, healthy fats, good-quality meat and fish, gluten-free grains and nuts and seeds. You'll find that you don't think about food as much, that you can sit back and enjoy your life. Trust me, diets don't work, so stop depriving yourself and start living.

4. **Banish the beige:** Bread, pasta, pizza . . . yes, they're out. Why? Well, they're not whole foods. They're full of chemicals, preservatives and genetically modified wheat. Wheat makes up a lot of our typical Western diet: it's in bread, cakes, biscuits and it's also used to thicken sauces, soups and condiments. With it being in such high demand, it is now artificially manufactured, meaning it lacks any of the nutritional value it used to hold. Cutting out wheat means cutting out the crap!

5. **Three meals a day keeps indigestion at bay:** Often we eat way too much, snacking all day in an attempt to battle

our fatigue. But we don't need all this food: three meals a day – a good protein-rich breakfast followed by two wholesome meals – is adequate for most of us. If you have an active job or exercise a lot you might need an extra snack over the course of the day, but try to get in the habit of having proper meals. Leave at least a four-hour gap in between to allow your stomach to empty and your body to rest. After all, it works hard to transfer that quinoa salad into energy, so cut it some slack!

6. **Get on the chew-chew train:** It's time to start using our teeth. This may sound strange, but there is a reason why I've made this one of my nine principles. Most of us don't chew our food: we wolf it down on the way to a meeting, while checking emails or sat in front of the TV. But doing this means you aren't digesting your food or absorbing the nutrients efficiently, and neither do you register when you're full. Digestion starts in the mind, so get present while you're eating: no distractions, no eating and Tweeting. Sit down, breathe and chew your food 10–15 times: relax while you eat, don't rush. Watch your bloated belly disappear, your body feel calmer and your desire to grab something sweet diminish.

7. **Get your fats straight:** Ah, the terrible F-word: The thing we don't want to be and the foods we have long avoided. But fats are so good for you! They will make your hair shine, your nails grow and your skin glow. They are an amazing source of energy, keeping you full all day long. They boost your immune system and contain essential fatty acids that are vital for your body. Healthy fats play a crucial role in maintaining your health: fatty acids help absorb fat-soluble vitamins A, D, E and K. So up your fats from healthy sources like nuts, seeds, fish, eggs, olive oil, coconut oil and avocados.

8. **Getting meaty:** People are sometimes surprised that I cook with meat and fish. 'Isn't meat bad for you?', I'm often asked. Well, it's all about quality, and I always choose pasture-raised, grass-fed meat. Grass-fed beef is naturally leaner than grain-fed beef: it contains much higher levels of omega-3 fatty acids and is a great source of CLA (conjugated linoleic acid), a fat that reduces the risk of obesity, diabetes and many immune disorders. If you don't eat meat, no worries! But if you do, try to buy the best quality. It will be slightly more expensive so think buy less, buy better – use the money you would have spent on a few pieces of cheaper meat and just buy one that's good quality. The taste alone will get you hooked.

9. **Cook once, eat twice:** I hate washing up, so I cut corners by cooking an extra portion of whatever recipe I'm making in the evening for me to eat the next day. It means I have lunch ready and don't have to scrub an extra dish. It is a money and time saver, and one of my golden rules that I can't recommend enough! You'll see this added to the meal plans later in this book (see pages 246–51).

store cupboard essentials

Right, it's time to clear out your cupboards. Trust me, once your kitchen is filled with goodness, healthy eating becomes a breeze. I know this list may seem over-whelming and expensive, but once you have the staples, cooking these delicious and nutritious recipes will become easy and cost-effective in the long term. So stock up and get ready to glow!

nuts and seeds

almonds, almond butter and milk

This sexy nut is a staple in my cupboard. I like to put toasted blanched flaked almonds on top of salads such as my Fennel, Cabbage and Dijon-Spiced Slaw (pages 94–5), or blitz them in a food processor to make ground almonds or almond flour to bake with. Full of protein and skin-glowing vitamin E, these nuts are ideal for snacking on to curb cravings or to boost the nutritional value of your breakfast.

Almond butter is my favourite nut butter and it makes smoothies like Green Goddess Smoothie and Butter Cup Smoothie (page 46) super creamy. Nut butters are

becoming more popular and easier to find: watch out, they can be addictive! There have been plenty of spoons found late at night beside my jars.

My almond addiction doesn't stop at butter: I love almond milk, too. It's perfect for making porridge, using in baking and adding to green tea. If you are allergic to nuts, use rice or coconut milk instead.

cashews

I love cashews! Toasted cashews are my favourite snack, and you will spot them in a number of my recipes. If you are allergic, or just don't like nuts, replace them with a nice toasted seed. Cashews are a tree nut loaded with vitamin K (great for beating the eye bags), and are a healthy source of protein and fats. They can also be used to make dairy-free creams, which I use in my Banoffee Mousse (pages 228–9), and to make the base for raw desserts such as my Raw Ginger Crunch (pages 238–9).

chia seeds

Native to Mexico and Guatemala, these seeds were known for boosting the Aztecs' energy levels, due to their rich sources of amino acids, fibre and nutrients. You can buy them from wholefood stores and online, and I'm now starting to see them in major supermarkets due to demand. If you have never used them you are in for a treat! They are hydrophilic, meaning they swell up in

liquid to make a jelly-like texture. You can use them in puddings such as my Mango Chia Pudding (pages 68–9), and to replace eggs in some recipes, such as my Courgette and Halloumi Mini Frittatas and Spinach Bread (pages 158–9 and 180–1). All you need to do is mix 1 tablespoon of chia seeds with 3 tablespoons of water, let this sit for 15 minutes, stirring well (this replaces one egg; double the mix for two). You can also use it to make a gelatinous texture in jams: try my blueberry jam with the Lemon and Blueberry Overnight Oats (pages 70–1). It's delicious!

pistachios

This colourful nut always reminds me of summer holidays in Turkey. Full of healthy fatty acids and antioxidants they add a great crunch to my Pimping Porridge with Pomegranate (pages 66–7). Aim to buy the raw unsalted variety and then you can add your own flavour to them. The ready-salted ones often contain refined table salt instead of good quality sea salt.

pumpkin seeds

Also known as pepitas, these little seeds pack a punch with a big load of zinc, which is great for banishing pimples. They taste delicious, contain antioxidants and have antimicrobial effects (inhibiting the growth of bad bacteria in your gut). They make any salad come to life, and I love to bake with them, too. They give colour and crunch to my Baked Apple and Blueberry Oats (pages 178–9) and make a mighty snack. You can find them in supermarkets, health food stores and online.

quinoa

A very mighty pseudo-grain and probably the most popular in the health market right now due to its high protein content. Pronounced keen-wah (don't worry, it took me a while to get it!) it is actually more of a seed than a grain. It doesn't matter which colour quinoa you get, though the white is a little softer in texture and taste, which is why it is the most popular. Quinoa is a great staple in my cooking: it takes on a world of flavours in recipes such as my Magical Moroccan Quinoa Dish (pages 114–5) and can also be used in flake form (like oats) in my Coconut and Lime Quinoa Porridge (pages 56–7).

sesame seeds

Consisting of 20 per cent protein, these seeds are pretty super. They contain zinc, which helps to produce collagen, giving skin that youthful look. Toast them and add to dishes such as my Tuna Ceviche with Charred Lettuce and Avocado (pages 160–1) and my Smoked Salmon, Poached Eggs, Chilli-Spiced Yoghurt and Crispy Kale (pages 58–9).

tahini

If you're dairy-free this is definitely something to get into your diet. Containing a dose of calcium, iron, magnesium and zinc, it's a nutritional powerhouse. Make sure you stock up on this: I use it in lots of dressings – for my Grilled Halloumi and Mango Slaw (pages 88–9) and my Chickpea and Hazelnut Falafels (pages 120–1). When I need a quick snack, I'll chop up a carrot and an apple and dip them into some tahini with cinnamon. It's the dream.

walnuts

Walnuts are a soft, slightly bitter nut. They are incredibly versatile, working equally well with sweet dishes such as my comforting Walnut and Raisin Fruit Loaf (pages 174–5) as with savoury: try them in my Pan-Fried Sea Bass (pages 138–9). Walnuts hold the trophy for their high levels of omega-3 fatty acids, making them the brainy nut. Grab a handful to munch on at work when you need that extra brain boost to get through the day.

flours

buckwheat flour

Made from ground-down buckwheat (which is similar to quinoa), this is an ancient crop loaded with fibre and B vitamins. I love to use this flour in my gluten-free baking as it has a delicious nutty taste: it goes so well in my Baked Strawberry and Raspberry Tart (pages 226–7). You can find it at your local health food store or it can be ordered online.

rice flour

Another gluten-free flour, this is perhaps easier to find in supermarkets. This flour is great for baking cookies, muffins and cakes, and it also thickens sauces so you can get that lovely rich gravy for your Sunday roast. A great source of magnesium and manganese, you will love baking with this flour: it works in a similar way to ordinary flour, so you can replace it like for like in recipes.

grains, pulses and legumes

butter beans (canned)

A great source of protein, fibre, iron and B vitamins. I love cooking with them: they're delicious in my Vegan Full English (pages 182–3) and in my Butter Bean and Almond Dip (pages 102–3). They're cheap to buy, so I always make sure I have a few extra cans stashed away in my cupboard.

chickpeas

A legume, chickpeas are best known for making hummus, but they do so much more than that. Why not make my Chickpea Curry or Chickpea and Hazelnut Falafel (pages 118–9 and 120–1)? Such great vegan sources of protein, they also contain soluble fibre that helps regulate blood sugar levels so you stay full throughout the day. I love canned chickpeas because they're so quick to use, but you can also buy them dried and boil them up yourself.

lentils

This legume comes in many shapes and colours, but I like using red lentils as they are quicker to cook and have a lovely bright colour. You can also buy them pre-prepared in cans, which saves a little time. Rich in folate, zinc and B vitamins, they work well in warm salads such as my Roasted Cauliflower and Spiced Lentils (pages 220–1), and in soups – try my Red Thai Sweet Potato and Lentil Soup (pages 80–1).

oats

Oats are such a staple in my cupboard; I love using them to make delicious breakfasts, such as Vegan Oat and Banana Pancakes (pages 54–5). They are versatile, tasty and give your body a good dose of skin-glowing selenium. You can grind them down into flour, as in my Carrot Bircher (pages 50–1). Aim to grab the gluten-free oats, especially if you are sensitive. These are particularly good for digestion due to their high fibre content and they are pretty easy to buy in supermarkets and health food stores. Grab porridge oats for porridge and rolled oats for baking, as in my Baked Apple and Blueberry Oats (page 178–9).

spices and flavourings

cayenne pepper

This is such a brilliant spice to cook with – a little really goes a long way and its fiery red colour makes every dish look gorgeous. Cayenne pepper stimulates the digestive tract, helping to aid food digestion and keep your gut healthy! A curry isn't a curry without it, and I use it to give a kick to both my Goan Chicken Curry (pages 130–1) and Chickpea Curry (pages 118–9).

chilli powder/chilli flakes

These little babies are potent flavour in a pinch! Chilli is known to be seriously anti-inflammatory, which can help in fighting many diseases. Even more usefully, chilli flakes have been found to stabilise blood sugar levels, which we all know is just amazing. Sprinkle these over salads like my Grilled Halloumi and Mango Slaw (pages 88–9) to elevate them to the next level!

cinnamon

This is your best friend if you get sugar cravings. It contains antioxidant properties that protect the body from oxidative damage caused by free radicals such as sun damage, pollution and a poor diet. Add it to sweeten your morning porridge or to liven up your Black Bean Shepherd's Pie (pages 206–7).

cumin seeds

These little seeds may look ordinary but they are one of my all-time favourite spices. They are super-high in iron, which is important to keep our blood healthy. You'll typically find this spice used in curry but I've also added it to my Lamb Cutlets with Salsa Verde (pages 164–5) and Chicken Kebabs with Cashew Satay (pages 218–9). Delicious!

garlic

This household staple has antimicrobial, antibacterial and antiviral benefits. It helps with iron absorption and gives a boost of sulfur that is incredible for the skin. Use it with roasted veg and in soups and stews. You will find it is one of the main flavourings in many of my dishes.

ginger

This super root is an incredible digestive booster and helps with nausea by soothing the digestive tract. It brings Asian dishes to life; I use it in my

Whole Baked Asian Fish with Bok Choy (pages 136–7) and in Chickpea Curry (pages 118–9). Store it in the fridge, along with your fresh chilli.

smoked paprika

An amazing ingredient to spice things up! It is full of glow-boosting antioxidants and contains vitamin E, essential for healthy blood-vessel function. It tastes amazing in Mexican, Italian, Indian, Moroccan and Thai dishes – everything, in fact! You'll always find this in my kitchen and I sneak it into lots of recipes, including my melt-in-the-mouth Beef Brisket with BBQd Charred Corn (pages 208–9) or a Vegan Full English (pages 182–3).

turmeric

Invest in turmeric rather than expensive superfoods such as spirulina and goji berries; this is the number one health food. Packed full of antioxidants and inflammatory properties, turmeric has been linked to cancer prevention and improving irritable bowel disease. It tastes divine in my Turmeric Milk (page 43) and I love mixing it into my Roasted Cauliflower and Spiced Lentils (pages 220–1). Be careful, though, as it stains everything!

sea salt

Salt isn't bad for you per se; it's all about the quality of the salt. Sea salt and Himalayan salt are full of minerals and natural remedies. Steer clear of table salt – this is bleached and highly processed. Buy yourself a nice bag of sea salt, a little goes a long way. Sea salt is pretty easy to find in all shops, while Pink Himalayan salt might be one for health food stores.

vanilla extract

Vanilla extract is one of the most important ingredients in my cupboard, especially when you can't get a fresh pod. I use this in so many of my sweet treats, such as my Heavenly Hidden Cake (pages 244–5), to heighten all of the flavours; it tastes rich and warm, so add it to smoothies and shakes to give them a delicious flavour!

oils, sauces and vinegars

apple cider vinegar

This amazing vinegar contains antibacterial properties that help reduce sore throats and sinus congestion. It is incredibly healing for your digestion: if this is your weak point try taking 1 tablespoon of apple cider vinegar before every meal. It can really help aid digestion and acid reflux. I love to use it in my dressings; it gives a good kick to my Fennel, Cabbage and Dijon-Spiced Slaw (pages 94–5) and my Spinach Bread (pages 180–1).

butter

Butter has been a staple in our diets for thousands of years and is rich in vitamin A, which is necessary for thyroid and adrenal health, lauric acid, vitamins E, K and selenium. It's a great stable oil to cook and bake with. Aim to buy organic butter as it's from cows that are pasture-raised and fed on grass, meaning the butter is packed with more nutrients and fewer chemicals. Store this beauty in the fridge.

coconut oil

Extracted or pressed from the flesh of a coconut, this oil is solid at room temperature and is great for cooking with as it has a high smoking point. Try to get organic cold-pressed oil and stay away from any pots that say 'hydrogenated'. I love coconut oil and you will see it pop up a lot in my recipes. It adds a nice coconut finish to raw desserts and tastes so good in curries. Store it in your cupboard snuggled up with your other oils.

dijon mustard

Dijon mustard is seriously underrated – it contains selenium for your skin, magnesium for your muscles and is rich in omega-3 fatty acids, so it is an amazing condiment to slather on veggies, or just to mix into dips if using it neat is too hardcore! It also acts as a great glaze for my Whole Apricot-Glazed Chicken (pages 196–7) and the sauce to my Slow-Roast Beef Cheeks with Celeriac Mash (pages 200–1) wouldn't be complete without it.

extra virgin olive oil

Made from pressed olives, extra virgin olive oil has magical pain-relief properties thanks to Oleocanthal, an anti-inflammatory agent. It is also rich in monounsaturated fat, which is great for mental agility. Drizzle it over veggies, mix it in salad dressings and splash it over the top of soups. I prefer not to cook with it at high temperatures as it isn't as stable as coconut oil. It's best to store it in the cupboard away from sunlight; it loves the dark.

sesame oil

This is one of my favourite oils to cook with because of its high smoking point, which means that it's stable at higher temperatures. Because it is rich in zinc, sesame oil is amazing for your skin's elasticity and smoothness, so you can get the glow and keep it! It totally makes my Tuna Ceviche with Charred Lettuce and Avocado (pages 160–1) and gives that Asian feel to my Sweet Potato Noodle Salad with Homemade Teriyaki Sauce (pages 86–7).

tamari

Rich in vitamin B3, this gluten-free soy sauce is great for bringing a bit of saltiness to Asian dishes like my Sweet Potato, Quinoa and Orange Stew (pages 222–3) and my Malaysian Coconut Milk Laksa with Beansprouts and Pumpkin (pages 186–7). Drizzle it over steamed veg like broccoli and bok choy to make them a little more exciting.

tomato purée

Another simple yet gorgeous ingredient. I use tomato purée to make my Mexican and Italian dishes extra sexy. It's packed with antioxidants and vitamin A to make your skin glow – just make sure you choose the no-added-sugar version to keep the nasties away. Its concentrated flavour brings depth to my Chicken and Olive Tagine with Cauliflower and Date Couscous (pages 134–5).

sweeteners

apricots (dried)
I love dried apricots, they bring a little sweetness to a recipe and bind ingredients together. Aim to get unsulfured apricots: they are a little less bright in colour but still taste just as good and they don't contain any nasties. They are rich in potassium, iron and antioxidants. I use them to make my Raw Lemon and Apricot Bars (pages 104–5) and they sweeten my Coconut and Apricot Granola (pages 172–3).

coconut sugar
This beauty is made from the sap of the coconut tree, which has been dehydrated. It is my favourite sweetener to use due to its caramel-like taste. Loaded with 16 amino acids, zinc and calcium, it is the golden child of natural sugars. It can be used easily to replace refined sugar in recipes (just swap the ratios 1:1), but it is still sugar, so don't go spooning it into your mouth all day long. You can find this delight at health food stores and online, though I'm sure supermarkets will start stocking it soon. Once you have a cache in your cupboard you'll be whipping up my Cinnamon Sweet Potato Bread (pages 170–1) on a regular basis! Keep it tucked up in an airtight container so it stays fresh.

dates
Dates are the dream! Their high fibre content means they're so good for 'keeping things moving', and because dates are rich in magnesium they are awesome for easing muscle soreness. They're also so versatile – use them in your smoothie, such as my Morning Kick (page 44), raw desserts, such as my Raw Key Lime Mousse (pages 228–9), in baking, or just as a snack on the go. Yum!

honey
This sweet nectar is anti-inflammatory and the best immune-booster around. A little goes a long way and it's been a great help for my sugar addiction. I use it to sweeten granola bars and to add a little sweetness to my Jamaican BBQ Chicken (pages 216–7).

other essentials

coconut (canned and desiccated)
The perfect ingredient to make a mean curry: coconut milk gives a lovely creamy effect with a nice sweet finish. Coconut is incredible as it is antimicrobial and is great for digestion, skin and fertility. I always have a can in the cupboard to add to my favourite Lamb and Spinach Curry (pages 198–9). Look for coconut milk that contains the least ingredients, ideally just coconut and water. You can also get cartons of coconut milk, which is a lot thinner, and I often use it for smoothies and to soften my green tea. Desiccated coconut is dried and grated coconut flesh and can be used in raw desserts and to sprinkle over porridge. As you can probably tell, I'm a cocoNUT!

eggs
I love eggs; they are the most complete food out there. A rich source of protein, vitamin D,

selenium and minerals such as zinc, iron and copper, they are a great way to start the day, fuelling you with energy that will last. Cook them any way you like, just always buy good-quality organic/pasture-raised/free-range. Quality is key. Aim to eat two eggs four times a week. You will find lots of eggy breakfast recipes in this book and, of course, they're used in my cakes, too. They are medium-sized in my recipes, unless otherwise specified.

lemons

These citrus beauties are wonderful to add a bit of zing to a dish, plus they are full of vitamin C. Unwaxed lemons are used throughout my recipes.

sweet potatoes

These are one of my favourite foods and I eat them all the time! Sweet potatoes taste amazing and leave you feeling fuller for longer because they are slow-release carbohydrates, so there's absolutely no bloat. They go so well as a side dish – try my Roasted Sweet Potato with Flaked Almonds (pages 188–9) – or let them take centre stage with my Red Thai Sweet Potato and Lentil Soup (pages 80–1).

tomatoes (canned)

This is a staple of any household: canned tomatoes add that creamy tomato richness to savoury dishes. An excellent source of antioxidant and vitamin C, I always have them to hand while making my Life-Changing Spicy Tomato Soup (pages 74–5) or my Beef Brisket with BBQd Charred Corn (pages 208–9). Always try to buy organic where you can because they contain fewer pesticides.

kitchen equipment

Other than a couple of pots, pans and a good knife, a great attitude is your best tool in the kitchen! You don't need a kitchen well-stocked with fancy kit to make a masterpiece, but there are a couple of useful gadgets that might make life a little easier and cooking a little quicker.

blender

If you love your smoothies, get yourself a nice blender: Nutribullet make a great, reasonably priced and sturdy one that is quick to use and you can whip up your smoothies, cream your mash potato and make fresh coconut milk in it.

food processor

I am often asked what is my most-used kitchen gadget: the answer is my food processor. It makes cake mix, raw desserts and cauliflower rice in seconds. If you are a keen baker I'd invest in a more durable model: they come with a higher price tag but they last for years and over time the price per use will be nothing. I love Cuisinart, but Magimix and Philips also make some good-quality ones.

spiraliser

If you want to make courgetti (courgette noodles) and sweet potato noodles, a spiraliser is a very handy tool. You can buy them online and in most kitchen stores, but failing that, a julienne peeler or regular peeler can also achieve a similar effect.

a little advice on . . .

portion size

Look down at your hands, make them into fists and place them together, with your thumbs side by side. This is roughly the size of your stomach: try to keep to this portion size.

Below is a breakdown of the sorts of foods that should fill your plate. Choose one item from the first three columns, but when it comes to the green veg you can eat as much as you like! A word of caution, though: too many veggies can make you bloated, so it's best to stick to one to two fist-size portions per meal.

protein	fats	carbs	green veg (unlimited)
200g of chicken, lamb or beef	½ avocado	1 roasted sweet potato or 100g of roasted parsnip, pumpkin or other root veg	rocket, fennel, lettuce, watercress, spinach, kale, chard, etc.
200g of fish	1 tbsp of olive, avocado or sesame oil	1 banana or other fruit	
2 eggs	1 handful of nuts or seeds	200g of non-starchy veg, such as mushrooms, peppers, corn, etc.	
150g of vegetarian protein (cooked quinoa, chickpeas, lentils, etc.)		100g of grains (rice, buckwheat)	

overcoming overeating

Meals have become supersized over the years, with giant plates and portions becoming the norm. However, overeating also stems from how we deal with our emotions, with food often being used to comfort ourselves or to help us to react to stress.

I passionately believe in a mindful approach to eating. Instead of sitting in front of the TV, where you're focusing on the screen in front of you rather than what you're putting into your mouth, sit at a table. This will allow you to slow down and focus on chewing your food. That way you'll be able to recognise when you are feeling full. Multitasking while eating prevents your body registering that it is digesting food, delaying the signal that tells you when you've had enough.

If you're feeling blue, stay away from the cupboards: that tub of ice cream ain't gonna solve any problems! Instead, go for a walk, a jog, or have a shower to wash off your mood.

snacking

I don't believe in constant snacking; often it's done out of boredom rather than actual hunger. However, a good, protein-rich snack at 4 p.m. is an effective way to stop you reaching for that chocolate bar or cup of coffee. And if you exercise in the afternoon, you'll definitely need an energy boost.

So, choose things like:
- A small handful of raw nuts
- 1 of my Raw Mango and Coconut Bites (pages 104–5)
- 50g of smoked salmon with 1 teaspoon of olive oil and lemon juice
- ½ avocado with salt and lemon
- ½ apple with 1 tablespoon of almond butter
- My Green Goddess Smoothie (pages 46–7)
- My Turmeric-Tastic juice (page 38)

eating healthily while travelling

Whether it's for work or pleasure, being on the move and away from your kitchen can make eating healthily a tough call. To keep up the good work:

- **Think greens, greens, greens:** ask for an extra side of steamed spinach, broccoli or salad in restaurants to add to a protein-led main meal.
- **Avoid processed carbs such as sandwiches, bread and crisps:** I know they're convenient, but they will make you feel tired and bloated.
- **Take some supergreens with you:** spirulina tablets or supergreen powder give a great nutrient-packed boost if you're not eating as you normally would at home.
- **Exercise:** just because you're away doesn't mean you can't get active! Hit

the gym in your hotel or local area, go for a walk or do my yoga routine that you can find at the back of this book (pages 252–67) in your hotel room.

- **Get your sleep pack ready**: if you fly a lot, make sure you have some ear plugs, an eye mask and some magnesium citrate powder; all these will help you get a good night's sleep.
- **Pop some snacks in your luggage**: re-sealable bags of nuts, seeds or coconut flakes won't take up much room in your case, or you could whip up a batch of my Raw Lemon and Apricot Bars or Fig Granola Bars (pages 104–5 and 176–7). To be prepared is to be well armed!

how to stay motivated

Staying on the right track can be tough – life throws us so many curve balls that can undermine our best efforts – but these are a few pointers that have helped me on this journey:

- **Set yourself goals**: What do you want to achieve? To be healthy? Have glowing skin? Lose weight? Boost your energy levels? Find balance in your life? Decide on your own personal goal and measure your progress weekly.
- **Stay motivated**: Stick some Post-it notes with positive messages on your mirror, laptop, desk, fridge – wherever works for you – to give yourself a little shout-out. The background to my phone says 'smile', and whenever I turn it on that's

exactly what happens – I let off a big Cheshire-cat grin.
- **Silence your inner critic**: We are our own worst enemies. Stop telling yourself you're fat, ugly, sick and tired. The more you say it, the more you believe it and the more likely you are to stay in that place. Start turning those words into positive ones to motivate you to sip on that green juice rather than reach for that glass of wine.
- **Surround yourself with love and support**: Your tribe is key; get support from your family, friends and work colleagues. You're far more likely to succeed when people are cheering for you.
- **Have compassion**: Change takes time. Some people see results quickly but for others it may take longer. You are on your journey, not someone else's, and you should enjoy every day of it. Treat yourself with kindness and empathy.
- **Celebrate every success**: Even a tiny change in the right direction is great, whether it's less bloating, reduced cellulite, more energy or finding a new love for cooking. Any positive result is awesome – well done you! It's time to celebrate.

mindset

I'm always asked the same question, 'Do you ever just eat a Big Mac?' The answer is … no! I genuinely love the way I cook and feel totally satisfied with it. Now, I'm not perfect so I won't deny myself a beautiful French croissant when I want one, but 90 per cent of the time I eat the way I have laid out in this book. This way of eating is habitual; it isn't a chore, or something I have to think about or battle with, it's just how I eat. How do I do it? Well, first off I fill my cupboards with good food – having healthy food around makes it easier. I choose the foods that I love and that taste good!

This can be you, too. You just need to change your habits! So keep going with your healthy choices and this new way of eating will soon become your norm.

how to get your loved ones involved

It makes life a lot easier when your other half and your family eat the same way as you do, and I'm often asked how I get my partner on board with my food choices. First off, you need to stop pushing your philosophy onto them. I know from my own experience that when I force my boyfriend to eat something that he doesn't like the sound of, he resists. Honestly, don't you hate being told what to do? The key is to lead by example, cook how you want to and casually drop in just how delicious it is and how good you feel . . . they'll soon follow suit.

At home I make a curry with white rice for my boyfriend and cauliflower rice for me. At first he turned his nose up at the veggie rice, but now he asks for it too! So don't see it as an issue, just make compromises and meals that you all enjoy.

how to boost your energy

Life can sometimes leave us all feeling a little flat, so you reach for the coffee, the sweeties or that glass of wine to pick you up. But the sugar in sweets and wine causes a high that is inevitably followed by a low, leaving you feeling more lacking in energy than ever. That's why all my recipes are free from refined sugar. Too much coffee can leave you feeling anxious and exhausted, too, so when it comes to coffee, it's all about not abusing it. That means sticking to one cup a day, before 11 a.m. Cutting down your caffeine intake can make you calmer as well as help you to sleep better and have more energy.

exercise and how to fit it in

Exercise is a great energy booster, so don't press snooze on that alarm – get up and go to that class! I used to let life get in the way of making time for exercise, but what has helped me is to schedule it in my diary as if it's an appointment I can't miss. Still, I know that we are living increasingly busy lives, so if you really can't make that gym class, start trying to increase your incidental exercise and move your body in other ways. It might be that you walk, cycle or jog to work, or get off a few stops early on your daily commute. Take the stairs instead of the lift, or volunteer more often to make the tea round! I find cleaning my apartment is a workout in itself. These little spurts of energy throughout the day really add up, so get going!

stress-free living

Stress is the big bad wolf, and it affects us all. It's hard to eradicate it completely, but you can learn to manage it. When it all gets too much, I find the best way to de-stress is to have breath breaks, where you step out of the office for some air. Think of it like a fag break, but with clean fresh air instead! Close your eyes and count to 4 as you inhale, then repeat as you exhale. Do this for a minute until you feel calmer, and repeat it as regularly throughout the day as you need to. Don't feel guilty about taking a time-out; we all need it.

Another stress buster is to connect with nature. When I lived in Australia, my world revolved around the sea. I would dive deep into that ocean and, as I did so, nothing else mattered. Back in London, swimming in the Thames isn't so tempting, so I often take myself for a long walk in one of the glorious parks that we're lucky to have in the city. Connecting with nature is so calming; whether it's a local park or river path or, if you live in a more rural area, woodlands or fields, or even the beach. Make a weekly appointment with Mother Nature and you will soon reap the rewards.

sleep

Sleep should be sacred and treasured. It is anti-ageing, it allows you to repair your body, reduce stress and control your appetite. But so often we feel restless at night and find it hard to switch off. Here are a few tips for how to get a good night's sleep:

- **Sleep regularly:** Stick to a regular sleep pattern, such as 10 p.m. to 6 a.m., or 11 p.m. to 7 a.m.
- **Ditch the tech:** Turn off technology and keep it out of the bedroom. No more late-night Instagramming, internet shopping or email checking. Put your phone away after 9 p.m. – anything on it can wait until the morning.
- **Cut out the coffee:** After midday, stick to herbal tea so you're not stimulated by the rush of caffeine.
- **Eat like your nana:** Finish dinner by 8 p.m.

so your body has enough time to digest it.
- **Turn upside down:** Place your legs up the wall: this yoga inversion is super relaxing. Breathe here for 5 minutes and feel your body melt.
- **Get some herbal help:** Drink some chamomile tea before bed, spray some lavender oil over your pillow and take some magnesium citrate – these will all relax you into a sweet slumber.

self love

I talked about this at length in *Get the Glow* because it is a topic I feel passionate about, and I've raised it again here as it is something that can be nurtured.

I want you to know that you don't have to be perfect; eating healthily is about loving your body and not about deprivation. You need to believe that you are enough, you are beautiful and you are amazing. This is so important. To reinforce this, I want you to practise these little examples of self-love each day:

- **Forgive:** Forgiveness is so important for self-love. You need to forgive your past mistakes, the times you've fallen off the wagon or done something you now regret. You also need to forgive others as well as yourself. If the past is weighing you down, remember: it's in the past, and you can't change it. Forgive and forget; you will be lighter and happier within yourself.

- **Shift the focus:** Focus not on what you don't have but on what you do have. Having more material possessions won't make you happy, so make note of the things you are grateful for: from the glimpse of a stranger's smile to the warmth of being with your loving family, to the delicious taste of a ripe and juicy mango on a summer's day. There are so many reasons to smile in this world, so let's focus on them.

- **Speak to yourself as you would like to be spoken to:** If you heard a person say to another, 'You're fat/ugly/old/stupid', you'd think they were terrible! So why, then, do so many of us say these things to ourselves? Let's start being nicer to ourselves and think, 'I am strong, happy and healthy'. Positive words affect how you feel, so treat yourself as you would your best friend.

FAST

smoothies

and

juices

turmeric-tastic

I'm obsessed with turmeric – the miracle antioxidant – it goes so well with the earthy carrot and sweet orange here. This juice is a total winner.

serves 1

2 carrots
3 oranges, peeled
1 knob of ginger, peeled
¼ tsp ground turmeric

Push all the ingredients except the turmeric through the juicer. Stir the turmeric into the juice and serve.

Will keep in the fridge for 1–2 days.

Please note: this is a juice, not a smoothie, so it should be made in a juicer, not a blender.

green is the new black

Yes, it is! This drink will leave you feeling amazing; it's packed full of the queen of veggies - kale - and brought to life thanks to the ginger and lime. You will become addicted to this combo.

serves 1
100g kale
¼ pineapple, peeled, cored and cut into chunks
1 apple, cored
1 knob of ginger, peeled
½ cucumber
juice of ½ lime

Push all the ingredients except the lime juice in the juicer. Mix with the lime juice and drink.

Will keep in the fridge for 1–2 days.

Please note: this is a juice, not a smoothie, so it should be made in a juicer, not a blender.

turmeric-
tastic

green is the
new black

skip to the beet

turmeric
milk

skip to the beet

This quick, fresh juice is tasty, healthy and the best colour ever. Be warned, if you're clumsy like me it's not the best juice to drink while wearing a white top!

serves 1
1 beetroot
2 carrots
1 apple, cored
1 knob of ginger, peeled
½ papaya, peeled
juice of 1 lemon

Push all the ingredients except the lemon juice through the juicer. Stir in the lemon juice and drink immediately.

Please note: this is a juice, not a smoothie, so it should be made in a juicer, not a blender.

turmeric milk

3
mins

My favourite winter warmer; the golden colour and softness of flavours makes this drink so delightful that I can't go a day without it.

serves 1
250ml almond or rice milk
½ tsp ground turmeric
1 tsp runny honey
¼ tsp ground cinnamon
tiny pinch of salt

Stir everything together in a small pan, bring to a simmer for a minute and then pour into a mug. Let it cool a little and enjoy!

Smoothies are the perfect quick breakfast, throw everything in, blend and go. Delicious, colourful and so fun to make, they are my go to breakfast when I'm in a hurry. All serve 1.

morning kick

300ml almond milk
1 shot of espresso, cooled
3 soft Medjool dates, pitted
pinch of salt
¼ tsp ground cinnamon
1 tbsp almond butter

Whizz all the ingredients together in a blender until smooth. This will last 1 day in the fridge but is best drunk fresh.

mango lassi smoothie

½ mango, stone removed, flesh roughly chopped
300ml rice milk
1 tsp freshly grated ginger
¼ tsp turmeric powder
1 tsp runny honey

Whizz all the ingredients together in a blender until smooth. This will last 1 day in the fridge but is best drunk fresh.

kiwi and vanilla shake

300ml coconut, almond or rice milk
1 kiwi, peeled and roughly chopped
1 passion fruit (just the inside)
1 vanilla pod, scraped, or ½ tsp of vanilla essence
1 tsp coconut oil
1 tsp runny honey

Whizz all the ingredients together in a blender until smooth and serve immediately.

morning kick

mango lassi
smoothie

kiwi and
vanilla shake

butter cup smoothie

2
mins

1 tbsp peanut or almond butter
1 banana
300ml almond or other milk
2 tbsp raw protein powder (I like Sun Warrior)
pinch of salt
1 tbsp raw cacao powder

Whizz all the ingredients together in a blender until smooth. This will last 1 day in the fridge but is best drunk fresh.

green goddess smoothie

3
mins

¼ pineapple, peeled, cored and roughly chopped
50g spinach leaves, washed
300ml coconut water
2 tbsp almond butter
juice of 1 lime
5 fresh mint leaves

Whizz all the ingredients together in a blender until smooth. This will last 1 day in the fridge but is best drunk fresh.

peaches and cream smoothie

3
mins

1 ripe peach, stone removed
250ml coconut, almond or rice milk
1 vanilla pod, seeds scraped, or ½ tsp vanilla essence
1 tsp coconut oil
pinch of ground cinnamon
1 tsp runny honey

Whizz all the ingredients together in a blender until smooth and serve immediately.

butter cup
smoothie

green goddess
smoothie

peaches
and cream
smoothie

breakfast

3
mins

(plus overnight
in fridge)

carrot bircher

Who loves carrot cake? Well, picture that taste in breakfast oats. The sweetness of carrots goes so well with antioxidant cinnamon and ginger. I love adding a sprinkle of coconut flakes at the end – it makes the bowl look picture perfect!

serves 2

1 carrot, grated
100g quinoa flakes or oats
30g buckwheat groats (or use 30g extra oats)
1 tsp ground cinnamon
pinch of ground ginger
1 tsp vanilla extract
1 tbsp honey
250ml rice or almond milk
2 tbsp toasted coconut flakes
2 tbsp pumpkin seeds
natural or coconut yoghurt, to serve

Mix the carrot with the oats, buckwheat, cinnamon, ginger, vanilla, honey and milk. Transfer to two jars or glasses and top with coconut flakes and pumpkin seeds. Place in the fridge overnight and enjoy in the morning with a dollop of yoghurt.

pea fritters with smashed avocado and poached eggs

Sometimes we need something other than bread to soak up that runny yellow yolk. My pea fritters are full of green goodness, and what breakfast eggs dish would be complete without avocado?

Blanch the peas in a pan of boiling water for a few seconds, then drain. Blitz the peas, spring onions, ¼ teaspoon of chilli flakes, the garlic, flour and 1 of the eggs together in a food processor with a big pinch of salt and pepper until chunky but combined.

Heat 1 teaspoon of coconut oil or butter in a frying pan and fry a palm-sized ball of the pea mix for a few minutes until golden, then carefully flip it over and cook on the other side in the same way. Repeat with the rest of the mix – it should make 4 fritters.

Grab the avocado, remove the stone and skin, place the flesh in a bowl and mash with a fork, then throw in the rest of the chilli flakes and the lime juice. Combine and set aside – the lime juice will prevent the avocado browning.

Boil about 400ml water in a saucepan, or enough so that the water is at least 4cm deep. Toss in the cider vinegar and a pinch of salt, keeping the water at a high simmer. Crack the eggs individually into small ramekins, then drop each egg into the pan of simmering water, a little apart, and poach for 2–3 minutes – or a few minutes longer if you want hard yolks. Remove with a slotted spoon.

To make the stack, for each serving, place one fritter on a plate, top with half the mashed avocado and sandwich together with another fritter, then top with two poached eggs.

You can prepare the fritters the night before and just poach the eggs in the morning. It's also a nice recipe to take to work in a lunch box.

serves 2

250g frozen peas
2 spring onions,
  roughly chopped
1 tsp chilli flakes
2 garlic cloves
70g rice flour
5 eggs
coconut oil or
  butter, for cooking
1 large avocado
juice of 1 lime
1 tsp cider vinegar
salt and freshly
  ground black
  pepper, to taste

15 mins

vegan oat and banana pancakes with strawberry and lemon compote

serves 2

100g oats
1 tsp baking
  powder
pinch of salt
½ tsp ground
  cinnamon
1 ripe banana
150ml almond milk
1 tsp vanilla extract
coconut oil or
  butter, for cooking
honey or maple
  syrup, for serving
  (optional)

Strawberry and lemon
compote
200g strawberries
grated zest and
  juice of ½ lemon
1 tbsp runny honey

I'm always looking for new ways to make sugar- and gluten-free pancakes. Oats are actually a really good way of substituting flour here as they grind down to a soft powder in a food processor. There's nothing better than smothering the pancakes in a juicy strawberry and lemon compote for the ultimate weekend breakfast!

Grind the oats down to a flour in the food processor then tip into a bowl and mix with the baking powder, salt and cinnamon.

Place the banana, milk and vanilla in the food processor and blend until smooth. Pour the wet mixture into the dry mixture and stir until fully combined. Let this sit in the fridge while you make the strawberry compote.

Roughly chop the strawberries and place them in a small pan with the lemon zest and juice and honey and let it simmer for 10 minutes.

About 5 minutes before the strawberries are done, heat 1 tablespoon of coconut oil or butter in a frying pan. Grab a few tablespoons of the batter and fry in the pan for a few minutes, then flip over and cook for a further minute until cooked through. Repeat with the rest of the mixture.

Serve the pancake with a dollop of compote and extra honey or maple syrup, if needed.

coconut and lime quinoa porridge with honey almond crumble

When we think of porridge, we think of winter, but this coconut and lime porridge will change all that. Quinoa flakes are a highly underrated alternative to porridge oats, and the tropical flavours in this version make this the perfect summer breakfast dish.

serves 2

2 tbsp runny honey
4 tbsp flaked almonds (or your favourite nuts)
120g quinoa flakes (or porridge oats)
400ml carton coconut milk (or your preferred milk)
grated zest of 1 lime
1 tsp vanilla extract or ½ vanilla pod
1 tsp coconut oil

Heat the honey in a small pan for a few minutes until it starts to caramelise, then add the nuts and cook for another few minutes until they turn golden. Take the pan off the heat and leave the crumble to cool.

Mix the quinoa flakes and milk with the lime zest (save a few pieces for the topping), vanilla and coconut oil. Cook for 5–7 minutes until cooked through (remove the vanilla pod if you used one), then top with the remaining lime zest and honey nut crumble and serve immediately.

8 mins

smoked salmon, poached eggs, chilli-spiced yoghurt and crispy kale

serves 2

100g smoked
  salmon slices
1 tsp sesame seeds
1 tbsp coconut oil
  or butter
1 lemon
1 red chilli,
  deseeded and
  finely chopped
50g kale, finely
  chopped
100g natural
  yoghurt
4 eggs
salt, to taste

Kale isn't something that people often think about eating for breakfast, but a cup of these superhealthy greens actually contains more vitamin C than an orange! Crispy kale is also great for mopping up egg yolk and is a good way to get more essential minerals into your diet.

Coat the salmon slices with the sesame seeds and transfer to a serving plate.

Heat the oil or butter in a frying pan, zest half the lemon into it with half the chilli and cook for 30 seconds. Add the kale and a pinch of salt, stirring well, and cook until the kale starts to wilt, then remove the pan from the heat.

Mix the yoghurt with the rest of the chopped chilli (to taste) and the juice of half of the lemon. Cut the other lemon half into slithers to serve.

Boil some water in a pan with a pinch of salt. When boiling, crack each egg into a ramekin then gently drop them into the boiling water, spaced apart, and cook for a few minutes until the egg white is no longer translucent and the middle is soft. Remove from the water with a slotted spoon and place alongside the salmon and kale. Serve with a dollop of the yoghurt and some lemon slices.

Don't leave your leftover kale to wilt in the fridge, whip up my Beef Burger with Tomato Relish and Kale Salad (pages 154–5) the next day.

beautiful breakfast salad

Breakfast salads are one of my favourite ways to start the day. I love mixing up my morning routine every now and then, and this dish helps me do just that. I prefer to fry my eggs in coconut oil; not only does it have a higher smoking point than regular oils but it also doesn't denature with heat. It makes the eggs super crispy, too!

serves 2

1 tbsp coconut oil or butter
4 eggs
1 large avocado, peeled and stoned
juice of 1 lemon
50g rocket
100g cherry tomatoes, cut in half
2 tsp chopped chives
2 tbsp good-quality pesto or leftover mint pesto (see page 152)

Heat the oil or butter in a frying pan over a high heat for 1 minute. Crack in the eggs, spaced apart, put a lid on the pan and cook for 1–2 minutes until the yolks are runny – or cook for a little longer if you prefer your eggs well done.

Slice the avocado and toss with the lemon juice. Arrange the rocket, tomatoes and avocado on a plate and top with the fried eggs. Scatter over the chopped chives and drizzle over the pesto to finish.

caramelised mushrooms and spinach with poached eggs and red pepper Romesco sauce

This is a super-simple recipe that you can whip up in minutes with no compromise on taste. You can make the Romesco sauce in advance and just pop it on your eggs in the morning.

Place all the Romesco sauce ingredients in a blender and blend until smooth. Set aside.

Heat the oil or butter in a pan over a medium–high heat, add the mushrooms and cook for 2 minutes. Throw over some salt and pepper.

Place the spinach in a colander and pour over a little boiling water to wilt. Leave to drain.

Add the garlic, thyme, chilli and balsamic vinegar to the mushrooms and stir for 30 seconds, then add the drained spinach and cook for another minute or two. Turn off the heat and cover the pan.

Meanwhile, boil a pan of water with a pinch of salt then turn down to a high simmer. Crack the eggs into ramekins one by one and gently tip into the simmering water. Poach the eggs for 2–3 minutes or until cooked to your liking.

Toast the bread and top with the mushrooms and eggs, then pour over the Romesco sauce.

Leftover Romesco can be drizzled over salads or dipped into with crudités. It keeps in the fridge for 5 days.

serves 2

1 tsp coconut oil
   or butter
100g mushrooms, cut
   into 0.5cm slices
100g spinach leaves,
   washed
1 garlic clove, crushed
1 tsp dried thyme
pinch of chilli flakes
½ tbsp balsamic
   vinegar
4 eggs
2 slices of rye,
   sourdough or gluten-
   free bread
salt and freshly ground
   black pepper, to taste

for the Romesco sauce
juice of 1 lime
80ml olive oil
1 red chilli
4 jar roasted red
   peppers in
   olive oil
20g toasted flaked
   almonds (or
   hazelnuts)
1 garlic clove
¾ tsp salt
2 spring onions,
   roughly chopped

avocado on toast with tomato, feta and mint

Tomatoes are a great breakfast choice; they are an amazing source of vitamin C (which is great if you're feeling on the verge of a cold) and potassium. Wake your body up to this balanced breakfast complete with protein-rich feta and skin-glowing avocado.

serves 2

1 tbsp chopped fresh mint
1 tsp sesame seeds
½ tsp ground cumin
¼ tsp ground oregano
1 large or 2 small avocado, peeled and stoned
50g feta
1 lemon, ½ juiced, ½ cut into wedges
2 slices rye, sourdough or gluten-free bread
1 ripe beef tomato, cut into 1cm slices
salt and freshly ground black pepper, to taste

Mix the mint, sesame seeds, cumin and oregano in a bowl with a big pinch of salt. Cut up the avocado into chunks, tear up the feta and throw both in with the spices. Mix well and coat with the lemon juice.

Toast the bread and place the tomato slices on top, then add the avocado and feta mix. Season with salt and pepper and serve with the lemon wedges.

pimping porridge with pomegranate, poached pears and pistachios

This fruity winter porridge combines some of my favourite sweet flavours. Pomegranate is known for its anti-inflammatory effects, but it also adds little pops of sweetness to this delicious dish.

serves 1

60g rolled oats
300ml milk
½ tsp ground cinnamon
1 tsp runny honey or maple syrup
½ tsp vanilla extract
pinch of salt
1 ripe pear, cored
1 pomegranate
1 tbsp pistachios

Heat the oats, milk, cinnamon, honey or maple syrup and vanilla together with a pinch of salt on a medium heat. Grate the pear into the oats and mix well, then cook for 5–7 minutes until the oats are cooked through.

Cut the pomegranate in half and take out the seeds of one half (leave the other for tomorrow's brekky!). Crush the pistachios with a wooden spoon or pestle and mortar until the size of breadcrumbs.

Spoon the porridge into a bowl, stir in the pomegranate seeds and scatter over the pistachios.

If you want to eat this porridge cold you can soak the oats overnight in the milk, honey and spices. It keeps covered for a few days in the fridge so you can prep a few bowls for the week ahead.

mango and sunflower seed chia pudding

The perfect summer breakfast. This tropical-inspired chia pudding tastes as amazing as a sunny day makes you feel. Chia seeds absorb their weight in water, so this will leave you feeling both full and hydrated!

serves 2

1 mango, peeled and stoned
juice of ½ lime
240ml almond or rice milk
50g chia seeds
2 tbsp sunflower seeds

Place the mango flesh in the blender with the lime juice and the milk, blend until smooth, then add the chia seeds and blend again. Pour into two small ramekins or glasses and place in the fridge to soak for 15 minutes. Stir every 5 minutes so that all the seeds swell.

Heat a small dry frying pan to a medium–high heat and toast the sunflower seeds for a minute, shaking the pan to prevent them burning, then transfer to a plate and leave to cool. Once cool, scatter the seeds over the chia pots.

5
mins

(plus overnight
in fridge)

lemon and blueberry overnight oats with blueberry jam and pistachios

It's no secret that lemon and blueberry are a match made in heaven. I've made this antioxidant blueberry jam by mixing together hydrating chia seeds and sweet honey, which will give your skin a superboost.

serves 2

150g rolled oats
350ml almond milk
1½ tbsp honey
1 tsp vanilla powder or extract
grated zest of 1 lemon
½ tsp ground cinnamon, plus extra for dusting
pinch of salt
100g blueberries
1 tbsp chia seeds
2 tbsp raw unsalted pistachios, roughly chopped
2 tbsp toasted coconut flakes or desiccated coconut

The night before, mix the oats with the milk, 1 tablespoon of the honey, the vanilla, lemon zest, cinnamon and a little pinch of salt. Stir well and divide evenly between two bowls.

Mash the blueberries in a bowl or blender with the remaining ½ tablespoon of honey and the chia seeds. Transfer to a bowl, cover and let it sit overnight in the fridge – this will form your blueberry jam.

In the morning, top each bowl of oats with the pistachios, coconut, a dollop of blueberry jam and a little dusting of cinnamon.

The oats and jam will keep for 2-3 days in the fridge, so you can prep a few of these bowls for the week ahead.

soups

and

salads

life-changing spicy tomato soup

When you don't have much time but still want a healthy meal, this is such an amazing soup to whip up. Make a batch in the evening and take it to work with you the next day, or freeze it for an instant lunch another day. It will change your life: maximum taste, minimum effort.

serves 2

1 tbsp olive oil
4 spring onions, finely chopped
2 garlic cloves, crushed
1 tbsp freshly grated ginger
1 tsp smoked paprika
1 tsp ground cumin
2 tbsp almond butter
400g can chopped tomatoes
400ml can coconut milk or vegetable stock
3 tbsp tomato purée
fresh herbs and seeds, to serve
salt and freshly ground black pepper, to taste

Place all the ingredients in the blender and blend for a minute until smooth. Add a big pinch of salt and pepper, blend again then taste and add more seasoning if needed.

Serve cold in bowls topped with fresh herbs and seeds. Here, I have used freshly torn basil, a few extra chopped spring onions and pumpkin seeds, but freshly chopped coriander also works well.

Keeps in the fridge for a few days.

Jamaican squash soup

serves 4

2 tbsp coconut oil
6 spring onions,
  finely chopped
2 tsp allspice
3 garlic cloves,
  crushed
1 tbsp freshly
  grated ginger
1 red chilli,
  deseeded and
  chopped
1 butternut squash,
  peeled and grated
2 beef tomatoes,
  finely chopped
400ml can coconut
  milk
500ml chicken or
  vegetable stock
juice of 1 lime
1 tsp runny honey
crushed cashews
  and pumpkin
  seeds, to serve
salt and freshly
  ground black
  pepper, to taste

Butternut squash is seriously the dream soup ingredient. Not only does it go so well with spices, but its nutritional benefits make it a bona fide superfood, too. Butternut squash contains significant amounts of potassium, which is important for bone health, as well as vitamin B6, which is essential for both the immune and nervous systems. Whip up a batch of this super soup when you feel a cold coming on to fire up that immune system!

Heat the coconut oil in a pan and add the spring onions, allspice, garlic, ginger and chilli. Cook, stirring, for 5 minutes – if the garlic starts to burn, add a little water.

Throw in the grated squash, stir well and cook for a few minutes, then add the tomatoes with the coconut milk, a big pinch of salt and pepper and the stock. Bring to the boil then cook for 20 minutes until cooked through. Transfer to a blender and blend until smooth. Then stir in the lime juice and honey.

Heat in a clean pan – if you want it piping hot – then serve in bowls topped with cashews and pumpkin seeds.

courgetti prawn soup

serves 2

200g raw king
  prawns
1 tbsp freshly
  grated ginger
1 tbsp coconut oil
2 tbsp green Thai
  curry paste
2 carrots, grated
400ml can coconut
  milk
200ml vegetable
  stock (or use
  chicken or fish)
2 courgettes,
  julienned or
  spiralised
1 red chilli,
  deseeded and
  finely sliced
handful of fresh
  coriander,
  chopped
  (optional)

When I'm feeling tired or as if I'm about to be ill, my go-to is some sort of noodle soup, and courgetti always hits the spot. Red chillies are amazing when you have a cold; as well as being an effective antioxidant – the compound capsaicin that is found in chillies (which is what makes them spicy) has antibacterial and anticarcinogenic properties. Grab a bowl of this when you're feeling down to beat that cold!

Wash the prawns, pat them dry with kitchen paper then roll them in the grated ginger to coat.

Heat the coconut oil in a pan, add the curry paste and fry for 30 seconds, then add in the grated carrots and cook, stirring, for another 30 seconds. Pour in the coconut milk and stock, bring to a simmer and cook for 5 minutes.

Throw the courgettes into the soup along with the chilli and prawns. Simmer for 4 minutes until the prawns are cooked and have turned pink. Serve in bowls scattered with fresh coriander, if you like.

red Thai sweet potato and lentil soup

serves 4

2 tbsp coconut oil
1 onion, finely
   diced
4 large sweet
   potatoes, peeled
   and cut into
   5cm cubes
4 garlic cloves,
   crushed
3 tbsp red Thai
   curry paste
1 tbsp freshly
   grated ginger
1 tsp ground
   coriander
2 tsp ground cumin
500ml chicken
   stock
400ml can coconut
   milk
500g red lentils
1 tsp tamari
grated zest and
   juice of 1 lime
handful of
   coriander, finely
   chopped
25g pumpkin seeds
salt and freshly
   ground black
   pepper, to taste

Sweet potatoes are an amazing source of energy.
I'll grab a bowl of this for lunch to help keep me going
all afternoon long. The perfect winter soup for lunch
or a light dinner.

Heat the coconut oil in a pan on a medium heat. Pop the onion into
the pan with a pinch of salt and cook for 5 minutes. Add the sweet
potatoes, garlic, curry paste, ginger, coriander and cumin and cook,
stirring, for 5 minutes so everything is evenly coated.

Pour in the stock, coconut milk, lentils, tamari and some pepper
and bring to a boil, then reduce to a high simmer and cook for
20 minutes until the lentils are cooked through.

Blend the soup in the pan with a hand blender then throw in the
lime zest and juice.

Serve the soup with the coriander and pumpkin seeds scattered
on top.

fish soup

White fish is a brilliant source of protein. It's light so it won't make you feel bloated, which is why it's so good as an ingredient in soup. It's also a great source of omega-3 fatty acids, so it will help boost your brain power!

Start with the salad. Finely slice the fennel fronds and set aside, then finely slice the bulb and mix it with the lemon juice and the vinegar to stop it browning. Set aside until the soup is almost ready.

Heat a tablespoon of oil or butter in a frying pan and throw in the shallots, garlic and thyme with a pinch of salt, stirring well until the shallots brown – make sure the garlic doesn't burn. Add in the diced tomatoes and sliced fennel fronds and cook for 5 minutes. Pour in the fish stock, bay leaf and tomatoes and cook for a further 10 minutes.

Heat a teaspoon of oil or butter in another frying pan and brown the fish chunks for a few minutes. Add in the prawns and cook until seared and they have turned pink. Toss both the fish and prawns into the soup, leave to sit for a few minutes with the lid on and the heat off.

While this is sitting, finish off the salad. Drain the fennel slices and toss with the rocket and olive oil.

Transfer the fish soup to serving bowls and serve with the salad.

serves 4

coconut oil or butter, for frying
5 shallots, finely diced
4 garlic cloves, crushed
1 tbsp dried thyme
6 beef tomatoes, finely diced
500ml fish stock
1 bay leaf
400g can chopped tomatoes
300g skinless white fish, such as cod, cut into chunks
300g raw prawns
salt, to taste

for the fennel salad
1 fennel bulb
juice of ½ lemon
1 tbsp apple cider vinegar
75g rocket
1 tbsp olive oil

30 mins

heartwarming pho

serves 2

1 tbsp coconut oil
  or butter
3 garlic cloves,
  crushed
1 tbsp freshly
  grated ginger
100g wild or button
  mushrooms,
  chopped in half
450ml chicken
  stock
1 tbsp tamari
2 star anise
1 cinnamon stick
1 large carrot or
  2 small, julienned
3 pak choi, cut
  in half
4 eggs
1 red chilli,
  deseeded amd
  finely sliced, to
  serve
2 spring onions,
  finely sliced,
  to serve

I love pho for supper; it's a Vietnamese-inspired soup with plenty of heartwarming veg. This is the perfect light meal for a cold night when you're looking to get loads of vitamins in one hit.

Heat the oil or butter in a pan, throw in the garlic and ginger and cook for 30 seconds, then throw in the mushrooms and stir-fry for 2 minutes. Pour over the stock, tamari, star anise and cinnamon stick and bring to a boil, then reduce to a simmer and cook for 10 minutes. Throw the carrots and pak choi into the soup to cook for a further 7 minutes while you prepare the eggs.

Gently lower the eggs one by one into a pan half-filled with boiling water and boil for 5 minutes for runny yolks and 9 minutes for hard-boiled. Drain and hold under cold running water to stop them cooking and to cool them enough to peel.

Ladle the soup into two bowls, slice the eggs in half and place on top of the soup. Throw the chilli and spring onions over the soup to serve.

When you come across the cinnamon stick or star anise, remove them: they are there to add flavour to the soup but not to be eaten.

sweet potato noodle salad with homemade teriyaki sauce

I often surprise myself by finding new things to spiralise, and this time I've been at it with sweet potatoes! They spiralise surprisingly well and pair perfectly with Oriental teriyaki sauce. If you can't go a meal without meat, try serving this with some chicken.

serves 2

1 tbsp sesame seeds
4 tbsp tamari
2 tbsp honey
1 tsp freshly grated ginger
1 garlic clove, crushed
1 tsp sesame oil
2 sweet potatoes, julienned or spiralised
2 carrots, julienned or spiralised
2 courgettes, julienned or spiralised
2 spring onions, finely chopped
1 lime, cut into wedges, to serve

Heat a small dry frying pan to a medium–high heat and toast the sesame seeds for a few minutes, shaking the pan to prevent them burning, until golden, then transfer to a plate to cool.

Heat the tamari, honey, ginger and garlic in a pan for 5 minutes until it reduces. Take it off the heat and stir in the sesame oil, then throw in the sweet potatoes, carrots and courgettes and mix well so that everything is covered. Cook on a medium heat for 5 minutes. Toss in the spring onions, top with the toasted sesame seeds and serve with lime wedges for squeezing over.

grilled halloumi and mango slaw with coconut tahini dressing

This is my dream summer salad; I love the sweet flavours of mango and fennel mixed with salty halloumi and drizzled with creamy tahini dressing. It's a real crowd-pleaser, perfect eaten al fresco on a warm evening.

serves 4
coconut oil or butter, for cooking
100g cashews
1 fennel bulb, thinly sliced, julienned or grated
1 carrot, thinly sliced, julienned or grated
1 mango, stoned and thinly sliced, julienned or grated
50g raisins
400g halloumi, cut into 1cm slices
10g basil leaves, torn, to serve
1 red chilli, deseeded and finely sliced, to serve
salt, to taste

Dressing
2 tbsp tahini
juice of 1 lime
½ tsp salt
1 tbsp finely grated ginger
1 tbsp coconut milk

Heat 1 teaspoon of coconut oil or butter in a pan, throw in the cashews and stir well to coat. Sprinkle over some salt and keep stirring for a few minutes until golden. Tip out onto a plate to cool. Mix the fennel, carrot, mango and raisins in a bowl. In a jar, combine the dressing ingredients, adding 1–2 tablespoons of water to thin it out.

Heat 1 tablespoon of coconut oil in a griddle or frying pan over a high heat, then grill the halloumi for 1 minute on each side until golden. Top the veggies with the halloumi and cashews and drizzle over the dressing. Throw over the basil leaves and chilli to serve.

7
mins

beetroot, kale and mozzarella salad

I don't often eat dairy, but when I do I make sure it's good quality. Mozzarella is a good source of veggie protein and is high in calcium, too, which is essential for beautiful bones, and I love the way this cheese goes with beetroot. Remember to chew, chew, chew the kale in this, as it is harder to digest when it's raw.

serves 2

1 tsp runny honey
3 tbsp olive oil
2 tsp apple cider vinegar
grated zest of 1 orange
1 orange, peeled and sliced
100g kale, stems removed and leaves finely chopped
2 tbsp pumpkin seeds
4 cooked beetroots, thinly sliced
125g mozzarella (one ball)
salt, to taste

Combine the honey, olive oil, vinegar and orange zest with a pinch of salt. Massage the dressing into the chopped kale for a few minutes until it starts to wilt. Transfer to a serving plate.

Heat a small dry frying pan to a medium–high heat and toast the pumpkin seeds with a pinch of salt for a few minutes until golden, shaking the pan constantly to prevent them burning. Tip them onto a plate to cool.

Scatter the beetroot slices over the kale, then tear the mozzarella and throw it over the beetroot. Peel the orange and cut the flesh into thin slithers, then throw these over the top of the salad and sprinkle over the toasted pumpkin seeds.

10 mins

roasted chicory, grape and dill salad

This luxurious salad is a showstopper. It's indulgent but so fresh and tasty. I love the roasted grapes – they burst with their soft sweetness, which teams perfectly with the chicory and mustard flavours. Salad just got interesting.

serves 2

1 tbsp coconut oil or butter
2 heads of chicory, halved lengthways, base left intact
200g grapes, halved and deseeded
1 tbsp runny honey
1 tsp Dijon mustard
100g goats' cheese
25g walnuts, roughly chopped
1 tbsp chopped fresh dill

Melt the oil or butter in a pan, add the chicory, cut-side down, and cook for 5 minutes. Turn over and add the grapes, giving them a stir, and fry until cooked through and softened.

Pour in the honey with the mustard, then give it all a stir to evenly coat the fruit and vegetables. Cook for another minute until warmed through.

Serve the chicory and grapes with the goats' cheese, walnuts and fresh dill scattered over.

10
mins

fennel, cabbage and Dijon-spiced slaw

I adore fennel in my salads; it's a super soother on the gut and here I've mixed it with purple cabbage to really boost your digestion. Serve this up as a side salad, too – it would go perfectly with my Jamaican BBQ chicken (pages 216–7)!

serves 6 as a side

100g flaked almonds
½ head purple cabbage, thinly sliced
2 fennel bulbs, thinly sliced
1 red onion, thinly sliced
2 apples, cored and thinly sliced
juice of 1 lemon
1 garlic clove, crushed
1 tbsp apple cider vinegar
250ml natural or coconut yoghurt
2 tbsp Dijon mustard
3 tbsp olive oil
3 tbsp chopped fresh dill
pinch of salt

Heat a small dry frying pan to a medium–high heat and toast the almonds until golden, taking care not to let them burn. Tip out onto a plate to cool.

Coat the cabbage, fennel, onion and apple slices in the lemon juice to prevent them browning.

Mix the garlic, vinegar, yoghurt, mustard, oil and dill together with a pinch of salt and stir it into the veg. Give it a good massage to coat, then serve scattered with the toasted almond flakes.

mango and avocado salad

I adore the taste and texture of this fruit and veg combo – the juicy mango and creamy avocado go so well together. It's a great salad to beat the bloat; mango is beneficial for digestion as it contains prebiotic dietary fibre that feeds the good bacteria in your gut that help break down food.

serves 4 as a side

50g cashews
1 mango, peeled and stoned
1 avocado, peeled and stoned
juice of 2 limes
1 red chilli, finely sliced (deseeded, if you like)
1 tsp freshly grated ginger
50g rocket
2 tbsp finely chopped mint

Heat a small dry frying pan to a medium–high heat and toast the cashews for 5 minutes, shaking the pan to prevent them burning, until browned. Tip onto a plate to cool.

Finely slice the mango and avocado and toss in half of the lime juice to prevent them browning.

Mix the remaining lime juice with the chilli and ginger. Pile up the rocket, mango and avocado in the middle of a plate, throw over the toasted cashews, drizzle over the spicy dressing and scatter over the chopped mint.

shredded Thai chicken salad with toasted cashews

serves 2

2 skinless and
  boneless chicken
  breasts
1 tsp turmeric
1 red chilli,
  deseeded and
  finely chopped,
  plus extra to serve
  (optional)
1 tbsp freshly
  grated ginger
grated zest and
  juice of 1 lime
25g cashew nuts
1 tbsp coconut oil
  or butter
2 little gem
  lettuces, shredded
4 spring onions,
  finely chopped
100g sugar snap
  peas, finely
  chopped
2 tbsp olive oil
10g fresh basil
  leaves, finely
  chopped
salt, to taste

This protein-packed salad will bring a taste of Thailand to your kitchen. Top with toasted cashews for a punch of magnesium, which is great for heart and muscle health. This is the perfect post-workout meal.

Rub the chicken breasts with the turmeric, half the chopped chilli, the ginger, the lime zest and a big pinch of salt.

Heat a small frying pan over a medium–high heat and toast the cashew nuts for a minute, shaking the pan to prevent them burning, until golden. Tip onto a plate to cool.

Grease a griddle pan with the oil or butter and set over a high heat. Cook the chicken on the hot griddle for 3–4 minutes on one side until bronzed then flip it over, turning the heat down to medium and cooking for a further 6–7 minutes until cooked through. Transfer to a plate to rest.

Place the lettuce, spring onions and sugar snaps in a bowl. Once the chicken is slightly cooled, shred it with your fingers into strips and scatter it over the salad.

Mix the lime juice with the olive oil and a pinch of salt and drizzle it over the chicken salad. Top with the basil leaves and a little extra chopped chilli, if you like.

Leftover cashew nuts? Why not make the Mango and Avocado Salad (pages 96–7) or the Chicken Cashew Stir-Fry (pages 126–7).

Leftover spring onions? Make the Sweet Potato, Quinoa and Orange Stew (pages 222–3) or Red Thai Salmon Curry (pages 148–9) or chop them up over your omelette in the morning.

grab

and

go

snacks

butter bean and almond dip with veggie crudités

I love inviting my girlfriends over for a big girly catch-up, and when I do it's always good to have a dip on hand to munch on while I get dinner together. This dip is so easy to whip up; it makes quite a lot, so you can prepare this at the beginning of the week and take it in to work as a snack, too.

serves 8 as a dip

butter bean and almond dip
400g can butter beans, rinsed and drained
2 tbsp almond butter
2 garlic cloves
1 tsp smoked paprika, plus extra to serve
2 tbsp olive oil, plus extra to serve

crudités
1 chicory, leaves broken up
1 large carrot, cut into sticks
1 red pepper, deseeded and cut into slithers
100g sugar snap peas, cut in half lengthways
sea salt, to taste

Place all the dip ingredients into a food processor and blend until smooth. Top with some more smoked paprika and olive oil to serve.

Place the dip in a bowl and serve with the veggie sticks. Sprinkle with sea salt, to taste.

raw mango and coconut bites

30 mins

makes 8 bites

200g dried mango
grated zest of
1 lime
180g desiccated
coconut
2 tbsp coconut oil
1 tsp freshly grated
ginger
pinch of salt
2 tbsp sesame
seeds, plus extra
for rolling

If you're not too keen on energy bites that contain dates, these are the perfect alternative. Not only do these bites taste like summer, they will satisfy your sweet tooth without giving you even a hint of processed sugar.

Soak the mango in a bowl of water for half an hour then drain. Place the drained mango and the rest of the ingredients, except the sesame seeds, into a food processor and blend until fully combined.

Mould the mixture into 5cm balls and roll each one in sesame seeds until fully covered. Place on a plate, cover and put in the freezer for 20 minutes to harden. Transfer to the fridge until needed.

These will last 2 weeks in the fridge.

raw lemon and apricot bars

10 mins

(plus 30 mins
in freezer)

makes 8 bars

grated zest of
½ lemon
250g apricots
200g whole
blanched almonds
1 tbsp runny honey
2 tbsp coconut oil
¼ tsp ground
cinnamon

I love the taste of apricots and, like lemons, they are bursting with antioxidants and contain essential fibre for digestion. The perfect partnership!

Place everything in the food processor and blend for 3 minutes until fully combined and almost a toffee texture. Spread evenly in a small 25cm square baking tin lined with baking paper, cover and put in the freezer for 30 minutes to set.

Once set, cut into bars and leave in the fridge until needed.

These will last 2 weeks in the fridge.

raw lemon
and apricot
bars

raw mango
and coconut
bites

smoked beetroot crisps

30
mins

There's something so British about a good old packet of crisps, so I've created these smoked beetroot crisps as a natural, healthier alternative. Their smoky flavour makes them so moreish and will have you bursting with energy!

serves 4
2 red beetroots, sliced wafer thin
1 tsp melted coconut oil
sea salt, to taste
1 tsp smoked paprika
1 tbsp fresh thyme leaves

Preheat the oven to 160°C/325°F/gas mark 3.

Place the beetroot in a bowl and mix with the oil so it is evenly covered. Transfer the beetroot to two large baking trays, making sure none of the slices are overlapping (you might have to do this in batches). Sprinkle over the sea salt, smoked paprika and fresh thyme.

Bake in the oven for 20–25 minutes until crisp. Let them cool, taste and add more salt if needed.

30-minute mains

beetroot crepes with hummus, rocket and avocado

The mighty beetroot is full of health-boosting benefits and has been proven to increase energy levels, lower blood pressure and improve brain function. Hummus and avocado are full of good fats that will keep you going all morning.

serves 2

160g buckwheat flour
1 medium beetroot, grated
1 egg
250ml almond milk
pinch of salt
coconut oil or butter, for cooking
1 avocado, peeled and stoned
juice of 1 lemon
pinch of sea salt
100g hummus
seeds of 1 pomegranate
handful of rocket

Combine the flour, beetroot, egg, milk and salt in a large bowl.

Heat 2 teaspoons of coconut oil in a small pan over a medium heat. Pour enough mixture into the pan to cover the base in a thin layer and then cook the crepe on each side for 1–2 minutes until golden and cooked through. Repeat with the remaining batter, adding oil as needed – this should make 4 crepes, depending on your pan size.

Thinly slice the avocado and sprinkle over the lemon juice and salt. Add a little avocado onto each crepe with a few dollops of hummus, a handful of pomegranate seeds and rocket. Roll up and enjoy!

beauty buddha bowl

20 mins

This is such a colourful dish. It's the perfect showstopper summer salad and contains loads of vegetables to keep you feeling full. I love using miso in dressings as it's made from fermented soybeans, which makes it great for healing your gut.

Zest the orange over the beetroot and carrot in a bowl, then mix together with the tamari and leave to marinate. Peel and cut the orange into 8 segments.

Heat the oil or butter in a pan, add the garlic and cook, stirring, for a minute. Throw in the chickpeas with a pinch of salt and stir-fry for 10 minutes.

Mix all the dressing ingredients together and add a tablespoon of it to the chickpeas when you turn off the heat.

Slice the avocado and serve with the beansprouts, orange segments, chickpeas and slaw, keeping each section separate. Drizzle everything with the dressing and scatter over the almonds.

serves 2

1 orange
1 beetroot, grated
1 carrot, grated
1 tsp tamari
1 tbsp coconut oil
  or butter
2 garlic cloves,
  crushed
400g can
  chickpeas, rinsed
  and drained
1 avocado, peeled
  and stoned
100g beansprouts
2 tbsp flaked
  almonds
salt, to taste

miso dressing
1 tbsp sweet miso
  paste
1 tbsp freshly
  grated ginger
1 garlic clove,
  crushed
2 tbsp sesame oil
½ tsp honey
  (optional)
1 tbsp water

magical Moroccan quinoa dish

30 mins

Moroccan cuisine is so amazing, it's full of flavour and I love the addition of magical 'jewels' such as raisins and pomegranate seeds. The rainbow of ingredients here combine to make a dish that looks and tastes great and is an excellent vegetarian source of protein.

Heat the oil or butter in a frying pan, add the onion and sauté for 3 minutes on a medium–high heat, then add the garlic and cook for another minute. Throw in the cinnamon, cumin, allspice and a big pinch of salt and stir well. Add in the quinoa, raisins or sultanas and boiling water or stock and cook for 12 minutes with the lid on until cooked through, giving it a stir halfway through.

While this is cooking, put the lemon juice into a serving bowl and grate the apple into it. Finely slice the avocado and add it to the apple and lemon juice, too, mixing well to prevent them browning.

Once the quinoa is done, top with the apple and avocado. Knock out the pomegranate seeds (I know it's laborious but it's so worth it!) and mix them through the quinoa, then drizzle over the olive oil and season to taste.

This dish will keep for 1 day in the fridge (a few more without the avocado and apple). It's ideal for lunch the next day.

serves 2

1 tbsp coconut oil or butter
1 onion, finely chopped
2 garlic cloves, crushed
½ tsp ground cinnamon
1 tsp ground cumin
½ tsp allspice
100g quinoa
30g raisins or sultanas
250ml boiling water or chicken stock
juice of 1 lemon
1 green apple
1 avocado, peeled and stoned
1 pomegranate
1 tbsp olive oil
salt and freshly ground black pepper, to taste

Middle Eastern apricot and pistachio cauliflower couscous

serves 2 or 4 as a side

1 cauliflower,
  roughly chopped
2 tsp coconut oil
  or butter
1 tsp ground
  turmeric
1 tsp ground cumin
½ tsp cayenne
  pepper
2 garlic cloves,
  crushed
1 tbsp runny honey
grated zest and
  juice of 1 lime
100g spinach
  leaves, washed
100g dried apricots,
  chopped
50g pistachios,
  roughly chopped
2 tbsp chopped
  fresh basil
2 tbsp olive oil
salt, to taste

You'll probably notice from my recipes that I love taking food inspiration from Persian cuisine. This is because the spices featured in the food have such amazing health benefits, particularly turmeric and cumin. They also add a wonderful fragrant flavour to the cauliflower couscous, which is one of my favourite gluten-free substitutes.

Place the cauliflower florets in a food processor and pulse to break them down into a rice-like consistency. If you don't have a food processor, roughly grate them so that they look like rice.

Heat the oil or butter in a large pan and add the turmeric, cumin, cayenne and garlic and cook for a few minutes until fragrant. Throw in the cauliflower rice and cook, stirring, for a few minutes. Add 2 tablespoons of water and keep stirring, then throw in the honey, a big pinch of salt, the lime zest and juice, spinach and apricots. Stir well so the spinach starts to wilt and break down, adding a little water if it needs it.

Serve the cauliflower couscous with the pistachios and chopped basil scattered over and a drizzle of olive oil.

This will last 1–2 days in the fridge.

Use any leftover pistachios on the Lemon and Blueberry Overnight Oats for breakfast the next day (see pages 70–1), and if you have any dried apricots why not use these beauties to make my Raw Lemon and Apricot Bars (pages 104–5)?

chickpea curry

There's nothing quite like a curry on a Friday night, but it's much healthier and actually quicker to make your own rather than ordering a greasy takeaway. I love using chickpeas as a substitute for meat; they make a curry surprisingly substantial and will keep you full without that awful 'I've eaten too much' bloat.

serves 2

1 tbsp coconut oil or butter
1 red onion, finely sliced
1½ tbsp freshly grated ginger
3 garlic cloves, crushed
400g can chickpeas, rinsed and drained
100g frozen peas
1 tsp turmeric
½ tsp salt
¼ tsp cayenne pepper
1 tsp garam masala
1 tsp ground cumin
400g can chopped tomatoes
2 tbsp natural yoghurt, to serve
2 tbsp flaked almonds, to serve

Heat the oil or butter in a frying pan or wok on a medium heat and throw in the onion, then cook for 5 minutes until soft. Add the ginger, garlic and a tablespoon of water and stir well, then stir-fry for 2 minutes.

Throw in the chickpeas, peas, turmeric, salt, cayenne, garam masala, cumin and tomatoes with 200ml water and cook for 20 minutes.

Serve with a dollop of yoghurt and the flaked almonds scattered over.

chickpea and hazelnut falafel with tomato and pomegranate salad

serves 4

1 tbsp coconut oil
  or butter
1 red onion, finely
  chopped
4 garlic cloves,
  crushed
1 tbsp ground
  cumin
1 tsp smoked
  paprika
50g hazelnuts
400g can
  chickpeas, rinsed
  and drained
90g porridge oats
8 tbsp tahini
2 tbsp olive oil
juice of 2 lemons
250g cherry
  tomatoes,
  quartered
seeds of 1
  pomegranate
½ tsp ground
  cinnamon
1 iceberg lettuce
salt, to taste

Falafel is pretty much a staple in my house. I love eating it as a light lunch as it's packed with energy-boosting ingredients. I've created this version using hazelnuts, which provide additional essential fats and protein.

Preheat the oven to 200°C/400°F/gas mark 6.

Heat the oil or butter in a pan and cook all but 2 tablespoons of the chopped onion for 5 minutes, then add 3 of the garlic cloves, cumin, smoked paprika and a pinch of salt and cook for a further minute until the garlic is bronzed and the spices are fragrant. Take off the heat and set aside to cool.

Place the hazelnuts in your food processor and blitz until they form a flour-like consistency (not too long or you will get nut butter). Transfer to a large bowl. Place the chickpeas in a food processor with the oats, 2 tablespoons of tahini and a teaspoon of salt, and process until the oats have been broken down, then add the onion and spices mix. Mould the mixture into small round falafels and roll them in the ground hazelnuts so they are fully covered, then place them on a baking sheet. Bake for 15 minutes, turning the tray every 5 minutes so the falafels are evenly bronzed all the way around. Drizzle the olive oil and juice of 1 lemon over the balls and set aside.

While the falafels are cooking, combine the cherry tomatoes and pomegranate seeds with the reserved red onion, mixing well. To make the dressing, mix the remaining 6 tablespoons of tahini, juice of the remaining lemon, 1 garlic clove and the cinnamon together with a pinch of salt and add 3 tablespoons of cold water to thin it out a little, if needed. Slice off the stem of the lettuce then remove 8 leaves and set aside. Into each leaf place a few of the falafels, a little tomato salad and a tablespoon of the tahini dressing. Wrap them up and enjoy!

aubergine stew with cauliflower rice

30 mins

Aubergine is a real taste of the Mediterranean, which makes it perfect for a light stew. This dish is great for a summer night in and is so easy to prepare.

To make the aubergine stew, heat the oil or butter in a pan and cook the aubergines with a big pinch of salt for 5 minutes until they turn golden brown, stirring every now and then. Throw in the red onions, harissa, garlic, cumin, coriander, cinnamon and a pinch of salt and keep stirring until the vegetables are well coated in the spices and the mix is fragrant. Add the tomatoes and cook on a medium simmer for 15–20 minutes, stirring every 5 minutes.

To make the rice, put the roughly chopped cauliflower into a food processor and process for a few minutes until you get a rice-like consistency. (If you don't have a food processor, grate the cauliflower using a box grater.) Heat the oil or butter in a saucepan over a medium heat for 1 minute, then add the spices and stir for 1 minute more until fragrant. Throw in the cauliflower rice and sauté for 5 minutes, stirring constantly, until cooked through.

Serve the aubergine stew with the rice, a dollop of yoghurt and some coriander scattered over.

The aubergine stew can be frozen or kept in the fridge for a few days.

serves 2–3

aubergine stew
3 tbsp coconut oil or butter
2 aubergines, cut into 5cm cubes
2 red onions, finely chopped
1 tbsp harissa
4 garlic cloves, crushed
1 tsp ground cumin
1 tsp ground coriander
1 tsp ground cinnamon
400g can chopped tomatoes
2 tbsp natural yoghurt
chopped fresh coriander, to serve
salt, to taste

cauliflower rice
1 cauliflower, stalk removed and roughly chopped
1 tbsp coconut oil or butter
1 tsp turmeric
¼ tsp ground ginger

turmeric chicken burgers with shaved courgette and chilli salad

Turmeric is the superfood of the moment. Its high level of antioxidants protects the body from free radicals and it is known to be a natural anti-inflammatory. When paired with cumin and chilli you've got yourself a Persian-inspired flavour-packed dish! I've used chicken here but you could mix it up and try other minced meat.

Combine the chicken mince with the turmeric, ¼ of the chilli, the cumin, mustard, juice of 1 lime, garlic and a pinch of salt. Mix well so all the chicken is coated in the flavours, then with your hands form the mixture into 4 patties.

Heat some oil or butter in a pan on a medium heat and fry the patties, cooking them for 5 minutes on each side until lightly browned and cooked through.

Mix the grated courgette with the rest of the chilli (or just a bit of it if you want it less spicy), juice of the remaining lime and the olive oil.

Serve the burger wrapped in the lettuce leaves with the courgette salad tucked in.

If you have lettuce left over, use it in place of the two gem lettuces to make the Thai Chicken Salad (pages 98–9). Use any leftover mint to make some fresh mint tea, or start your day with the Green Goddess Smoothie (pages 46–7) tomorrow.

serves 2

500g chicken
 mince
1½ tsp turmeric
1 red chilli,
 deseeded and
 finely chopped
1 tsp ground cumin
1 tsp Dijon mustard
juice of 2 limes
2 garlic cloves,
 crushed
coconut oil or
 butter, for frying
1 courgette, grated
1 tbsp olive oil
1 large cos lettuce,
 leaves separated
salt, to taste

chicken cashew stir-fry

A stir-fry is my go-to meal for a quick dinner when I can't be bothered to cook and need food now! Before you have even picked up the phone to call for a take-away, you could have pretty much chucked any veg you have left over in the fridge into a pan. It's a brilliantly quick dish that doesn't compromise on taste and leaves you feeling full and satisfied.

Mix the chilli with the tamari, ginger, garlic and sesame oil.

Place the coconut oil or butter in a large wok or pan set over a high heat, throw in the carrots, courgettes and pepper and stir-fry for a few minutes, then add in a tablespoon of the chilli sauce, stirring well. Throw in the chicken, spring onions, cashews and the rest of the sauce. Keep stirring for 5–7 minutes until the chicken is cooked through. Taste and season if needed.

Serve topped with fresh coriander and sesame seeds.

serves 4

1 red chilli, deseeded and finely chopped
4 tsp tamari
1 tbsp freshly grated ginger
1 garlic clove, crushed
1 tbsp sesame oil
1 tbsp coconut oil or butter
2 carrots, cut unto matchsticks
2 courgettes, julienned or spiralised
1 red pepper, deseeded and cut into matchsticks
4 chicken breasts, cut into 1cm strips
2 spring onions, finely chopped
100g cashews
4 tbsp fresh chopped coriander, to serve
2 tbsp sesame seeds, to serve
salt and freshly ground black pepper, to taste

FAST: 30-MINUTE MAINS   127

Chinese duck bowls

serves 2

2 duck breasts,
  skin on
1 tbsp Chinese
  5 spice
1 tbsp sesame seeds
1 little gem lettuce
2 courgettes, julienned
  or spiralised
juice of 1 lime
1 spring onion, finely
  chopped
½ red chilli, deseeded
  and finely chopped
salt and freshly ground
  black pepper, to taste

plum sauce
5 ripe medium plums,
  finely chopped
1cm piece fresh root
  ginger, finely grated
1 garlic clove, finely
  grated
½ red chilli, deseeded
  and finely chopped
2 tbsp tamari or soy
  sauce
1 tbsp honey or maple
  syrup

This is a great date-night dish. Cook this for your other half and they'll have googly eyes for you all night. A lot of people never think to make their own plum sauce but this version is super-quick to recreate, not to mention sweet and spicy. I like using any leftover sauce as a marinade for meat, especially on a BBQ!

To make the plum sauce, add all the ingredients to a medium saucepan on a medium-high heat. Bring to a boil and then reduce to a simmer for about 15 minutes. Blitz in a blender until smooth.

While the sauce is bubbling, score the skin of the duck in a diamond pattern, season with salt and pepper and rub with the 5 spice. Place it in a cold pan, skin side down, then turn the heat to high. When the skin is crisp, turn the heat down to a medium heat and cook for a further 10 minutes, flipping the duck on both sides so it is cooked to your liking. You are aiming for it to still be pink in the middle but not raw. Once cooked, leave to the side to cool.

Heat a small dry frying pan to a medium–high heat and toast the sesame seeds for a minute or two until browned, shaking the pan to prevent them burning. Tip onto a plate.

Once the duck has rested, chuck it back in the pan and sauté it for a few minutes in its juices, then transfer it to a bowl and slice it up.

Break up the lettuce leaves and pop them into individual bowls, throw over the courgettes and top with the duck, drizzle over the plum sauce and lime juice and scatter over the spring onion, chilli and toasted sesame seeds.

Goan chicken curry

serves 4

1 tbsp coconut oil
   or butter
1 onion, finely
   diced
2 tsp ground
   coriander
2 tsp ground cumin
½ tsp freshly
   ground black
   pepper
1 tsp cayenne
½ tsp ground
   turmeric
3 garlic cloves,
   crushed
1 tbsp freshly
   grated ginger
500g chicken
   breast, cut into
   5cm cubes
400ml can coconut
   milk
200g sugar snap
   peas, sliced in half
   lengthways
juice of 1 lime
cauliflower rice
   (page 123), to
   serve (optional)

This is a really quick curry that can be whipped up in no time at all and uses ingredients that you probably already have in the cupboard. So next time you forget it's your turn to cook dinner, wow your housemates or family with this flavoursome chicken curry.

Heat the oil or butter in a large pot then throw in the onion and cook for 4–5 minutes until browned. Add all the dried spices, 1 tablespoon of water, the garlic and ginger. Stir for a few minutes, adding another 1 tablespoon of water to prevent the spices burning.

Throw the chicken pieces into a wok or large frying pan and stir-fry for a few minutes until all the chicken has turned opaque and golden. Pour over the coconut milk, bring to a simmer and cook for 7 minutes over a medium heat with the lid on. Throw in the sugar snap peas and the lime juice and cook everything for a further 3–4 minutes until the chicken is cooked through.

Serve immediately with some cauliflower rice, if you like.

chicken fajitas

serves 2

1 red pepper, deseeded and thinly sliced
1 yellow pepper, deseeded and thinly sliced
1 spring onion, finely chopped
2 large chicken breasts, sliced into strips
1 tsp smoked paprika
½ tsp ground cumin
coconut oil or butter, for cooking
1 red chilli, deseeded and finely chopped
3 ripe beef tomatoes, diced
10g fresh coriander, finely chopped, including the stalks
1 tbsp olive oil
2 avocados, peeled and stoned
3 limes
150g natural yoghurt
salt, to taste

tortillas
2 tbsp ground flaxseed (flax meal)
2 tbsp warm water
90g chickpea flour (also called gram flour)
pinch of salt
160ml water
pinch of ground cumin

Fajita nights – everyone has them, but when you're trying to get the glow it's hard to pass on shop-bought wraps. I've managed to solve this problem by creating these delicious tortillas made with chickpea flour that take just two minutes to prepare. Whip these up for your family – they'll be so impressed and they won't be able to tell the difference!

First, get the tortillas started. Mix the flaxseed with 2 tablespoons of warm water in a bowl and let the mixture sit for 5 minutes.

Meanwhile, mix the sliced veg and chicken with the smoked paprika, cumin and a big pinch of salt. Place a griddle pan over a high heat and add 1 tablespoon of coconut oil or butter. Once hot, throw in the spiced chicken and veg and cook for 7–8 minutes, stirring occasionally, until the chicken is cooked through, the peppers are golden and the onions are caramelised.

Meanwhile, in a small bowl, mix three-quarters of the chilli with the tomatoes and coriander and pour over the olive oil, stirring gently to combine. Then make the guacamole. Mash the avocado flesh with the juice of 1 lime, the remaining chilli and a big pinch of salt. Keep the texture a little chunky.

Return to the tortillas. Mix the chickpea flour, a pinch of salt, water and cumin with the soaked flax mix, stirring well to combine. Heat a teaspoon of oil or butter in a small frying pan, then pour out 100–125ml of the tortilla batter so it just covers the base of the pan. Cook on a medium heat until the sides start to crisp. Flip the tortilla over, cook until cooked through and it turns a bronze colour, then repeat until the mix is finished. Serve the chicken in the tortilla wraps with a dollop of yoghurt, guacamole and tomato salsa, and some lime wedges on the side.

chicken and olive tagine with cauliflower and date couscous

30 mins

We love a good tagine in my house, and when it's cold outside this is such a comforting dish. Adding dates to the gluten-free couscous adds a bit of sweetness and will give you a burst of extra energy.

Place the chicken pieces in a large bowl and mix with the smoked paprika, cumin, cinnamon, coriander and a big pinch of salt and pepper.

Heat 1 tablespoon of the oil or butter in a large pan and sauté the onions and peppers for 3 minutes, then add the garlic and ginger and cook for another minute. Push the veg to the side of the pan and add another tablespoon of oil or butter and the chicken, scraping out all the spices from the bowl into the pan. Cook the chicken until bronzed all over, then stir the veg back in and add the chicken stock, tomato purée and olives. Cook for another 10 minutes then stir in half the lemon juice.

While the chicken is cooking, whip up the cauliflower couscous. Blitz the cauliflower florets in the food processor or grate them to a rice-like consistency. Heat the oil or butter in a pan with the cumin for 30 seconds until fragrant then add the cauliflower and sauté for a minute. Throw in the dates and cook for another 3–5 minutes, adding the zest and remaining lemon juice, stirring well until cooked through.

Serve the chicken with a pile of cauliflower couscous.

serves 4

500g chicken thighs or breasts, cut into bite-sized pieces
1½ tsp smoked paprika
1 tsp ground cumin
¾ tsp ground cinnamon
½ tsp ground coriander
2 tbsp coconut oil or butter
1 red onion, finely diced
1 red pepper, deseeded and thinly sliced
1 yellow pepper, deseeded and thinly sliced
1 orange pepper, deseeded and thinly sliced
2 garlic cloves, crushed
2 tsp freshly grated ginger
500ml chicken stock
3 tbsp tomato purée
100g olives, stoned
grated zest and juice of 1 lemon
salt and freshly ground black pepper, to taste

COUSCOUS
1 head of cauliflower, florets roughly chopped
1 tbsp coconut oil or butter
1 tsp ground cumin
50g pitted dates, chopped into slithers

whole baked Asian fish with bok choy

Often, we don't like to bake whole fish here in the UK because it's so convenient to pick up a pre-packaged fillet at the supermarket, but go to a good fishmonger, pick up a fresh whole sea bream and try this recipe. Fresh fish always retains more nutrients than pre-packaged fish and the texture and taste is incomparable.

Preheat the oven to 200°C/400°F/gas mark 6.

Rinse the fish with cold water, pat dry and make two slashes in the thickest part of the flesh on both sides. Rub the fish with 1 tablespoon of the tamari and the coconut oil or butter and coat well in the sesame seeds. Place the fish on a baking tray and bake for 20 minutes in the oven until just cooked through – the flesh should be opaque when pierced with a sharp knife.

Place 2 tablespoons of tamari, the ginger and chilli in a pan and heat for 5 minutes until the ginger and chilli soften, then take off the heat, stir in the sesame oil and leave to cool.

Steam the bok choy over a pan of boiling water for 2 minutes. Plate the raw spring onions and bok choi with the fish and pour over the chilli dressing.

serves 2

1 whole sea bream
3 tbsp tamari
1 tbsp melted
  coconut oil
  or butter
2 tbsp sesame
  seeds
1 tbsp freshly
  grated ginger
1 red chilli,
  finely chopped
  (deseeded if
  you prefer)
2 tbsp sesame oil
1 bok choy, ends
  sliced off
2 spring onions,
  sliced into
  matchsticks

25
mins

pan-fried sea bass with spicy butter bean stew

serves 2

2 sea bass fillets
2 tbsp coconut oil or butter
2 tbsp fresh rosemary, finely chopped
2 garlic cloves, crushed
1½ tsp smoked paprika
100g chorizo, finely chopped
1 red pepper, deseeded and chopped
400g can butter beans, rinsed and drained
200ml chicken or beef stock
salt and freshly ground black pepper, to taste

This is a great dinner in all seasons. The texture of butter beans and fish just go hand in hand. I've added chorizo for extra flavour here as its smokiness is amazing with fish.

Rub the sea bass with salt and pepper, set in a bowl, cover and leave to sit at room temperature.

Meanwhile, heat 1 tablespoon of oil or butter in a pan, add the rosemary, garlic, smoked paprika, chorizo and pepper and cook for 5 minutes until the pepper starts to break down and the chorizo crisps up. Throw in the butter beans and stir well over a low heat for another minute. Add the stock and let everything simmer for 5 minutes while you prepare the fish.

Heat a frying pan to a high heat with 1 tablespoon of oil or butter, then pan-fry the sea bass skin side down for 2 minutes. Gently flip it over and cook on the other side for another minute until just cooked through.

Spoon the bean stew onto two serving plates and top each with a sea bass fillet.

25
mins

flaked miso salmon with courgette and radish salad

serves 2

2 tbsp sesame
    seeds
1 tbsp sweet miso
    paste
½ tsp tamari
2 garlic cloves,
    crushed
2 salmon fillets
1 courgette,
    julienned or
    spiralised
50g radishes, finely
    sliced using a
    mandoline
10g fresh coriander,
    finely chopped

dressing
1 tbsp freshly
    grated ginger
½ tsp tamari
1 tbsp sesame oil
juice of 1 lime

This is a dish that's easy on the tummy. My old friend miso is super soothing on the stomach and the flaked fish is very light so it will leave you feeling satisfied but not bloated.

Preheat the oven to 180°C/350°F/gas mark 4. Heat a small dry frying pan to a medium–high heat and toast the sesame seeds for a few minutes, shaking the pan to prevent them burning. Tip onto a plate to cool.

Mix the miso with ½ teaspoon of tamari and the garlic. Rub this into the salmon, then place the fish on a baking tray and roast in the oven for 10–12 minutes until just cooked through.

While the fish is cooking, make the dressing by mixing together the ginger, ½ teaspoon of tamari, the sesame oil and lime juice and set aside.

Mix the coriander with the courgette and radishes in a large bowl. Pour over the dressing and massage it into the vegetables with your hands. Serve with the miso salmon and the toasted sesame seeds scattered over.

sticky Asian prawns with quinoa and peanuts

20 mins

In some Asian restaurants the word 'sticky' on the menu also often means packed with sugar, because that consistency tends to come from the processed sweet stuff. Here, I've recreated this texture using sugar-free ingredients, with amazing results in both flavour and texture.

Mix the garlic, ginger, tamari, honey, half of the chopped chilli, the sesame oil and cider vinegar together well. Place 1 tablespoon of the sauce into a bowl and mix in the prawns, then leave to marinate at room temperature while you prepare the quinoa.

Wash the quinoa in a sieve then tip it into a pan with 250ml of boiling water and a pinch of salt. Cook for 12 minutes with the lid on until all the water has evaporated and the quinoa is cooked through. (If you are cooking brown rice, cook it according to the packet instructions.)

Heat a small dry frying pan to a medium–high heat and toast the sesame seeds and nuts for a few minutes, shaking the pan to prevent them burning. Tip onto a plate to cool.

A few minutes before the quinoa is finished, heat 1 tablespoon of oil or butter in the pan you used for toasting the seeds and nuts and throw in the prawns. Stir-fry for a few minutes until cooked through.

Serve the quinoa topped with the prawns drizzled in the sticky dressing and with the sesame seeds, nuts, raw spring onions and the remaining chopped chilli scattered over. Drizzle over the lime juice.

serves 2

4 garlic cloves, crushed
2 tbsp freshly grated ginger
4 tsp tamari
2 tbsp runny honey
1 chilli, deseeded and chopped
4 tbsp sesame oil
1 tsp apple cider vinegar
250g raw prawns
100g quinoa (or brown rice)
1 tbsp sesame seeds
50g peanuts or cashews
1 tbsp coconut oil or butter
2 spring onions, finely chopped
juice of 1 lime
salt, to taste

crispy mackerel with green bean, pea and coconut salad

20 mins

If you're in a rush you can use pre-cooked mackerel here, but I love using fresh fish for this – the texture is so much nicer and it's actually surprisingly inexpensive.

Sprinkle the mackerel with a pinch of salt.

Toast the coconut in a dry frying pan for a minute or two, then tip out onto a plate to cool.

Heat ½ tablespoon of oil in a pan and sauté the onion and chilli for 5 minutes with a pinch of salt.

While this is cooking, boil a pan of water and cook the green beans for 3 minutes until just tender. Drain. Add the peas and green beans to the onion mix and cook for another few minutes to cook the peas through.

Heat a pan on a medium heat with 1 tablespoon of oil and the curry powder and cook for 30 seconds until it becomes fragrant, then add the mackerel and cook, skin side down, making sure the curry mix covers the mackerel. Cook for 2 minutes, then flip over and cook for 1 minute on the other side.

Mix the pea, bean and onion mix with the coriander, olive oil, lime zest and juice and pile onto two plates. Place the mackerel on top and sprinkle over the toasted coconut.

serves 2

4 mackerel fillets
2 tbsp coconut flakes or desiccated coconut
1½ tbsp coconut oil
1 red onion, finely diced
1 red chilli, deseeded and finely chopped
200g green beans, trimmed
100g frozen peas
1 tsp curry powder
10g fresh coriander, chopped
1 tbsp olive oil
grated zest and juice of 1 lime
salt, to taste

pan-fried trout with cucumber, apple and dill salad

20 mins

The sweetness of the apple really goes well with this strong-flavoured fish, but if you can't find trout fillets you could use salmon instead. Although capers are known to be high in sodium, they add an extra burst of flavour, which is just what the fish needs.

Place the cucumber slices in a colander, sprinkle with salt and let them sit to draw out the excess water for 10–15 minutes while you prepare the rest of the dish.

Make the dressing by mixing the mustard, dill, vinegar and olive oil together with a pinch of salt. Thinly slice the avocado and apple and throw into the dressing to stop them browning, along with the shallots, stirring well to combine.

Heat the oil or butter in a frying pan on a medium heat, throw in the capers and stir for 30 seconds then move them to the edges of the pan and throw in the trout, skin side down. Sprinkle over a little salt and cook for 5 minutes until the skin is crisp, then flip the fish over and fry for another minute or so until almost cooked through. The cooking time will depend on the thickness of the fillet, but look for golden skin, a bronzed top and flesh that is opaque all the way through.

Rinse the cucumber, drain and then pat dry with some kitchen paper and mix in with the salad.

Divide the salad among two plates and serve with the fish and a sprinkle of capers.

serves 2

1 cucumber, peeled, halved and cut into ½cm semicircles
1 tbsp Dijon mustard
1 tbsp fresh dill, chopped (or 1 tsp dried)
1 tbsp apple cider vinegar
2 tbsp olive oil
1 large avocado, peeled and stoned
1 apple, peeled and cored
1 shallot, finely minced
1 tbsp coconut oil or butter
2 tbsp capers, plus extra to serve
2 trout fillets
salt, to taste

red Thai salmon curry

People often don't think to use salmon in a red Thai curry, but it's actually very tasty, and spiralised courgettes make the ultimate noodle to accompany this. If you have any left over, this is ideal for a warming Tupperware lunch in winter.

serves 2

1 tbsp coconut oil or butter
2 tbsp red Thai curry paste
2 garlic cloves, crushed
1 tbsp freshly grated ginger
400ml can coconut milk
2 courgettes, julienned or spiralised
100g mangetout, sliced into matchsticks
2 skinless salmon fillets, cut into 5cm cubes
2 spring onions, roughly chopped
1 red chilli, deseeded and finely chopped

Heat the oil or butter in a pan on a medium heat and add the curry paste, garlic and ginger and stir for 30 seconds. Pour in the coconut milk and cook for a few minutes, stirring well.

Toss the courgettes and the mangetout into the coconut milk mix, stirring well. Stir in the salmon chunks, pop the lid on and cook on a low simmer for 5 minutes.

Serve the curry with the spring onions and chilli scattered over.

25
mins

pan-roasted sea bass with broccoli mash, walnuts and capers

serves 2

2 sea bass fillets
2 tbsp walnuts,
  chopped
1 tbsp capers
2 tbsp coconut oil
  or butter
1 onion, finely
  diced
2 garlic cloves,
  crushed
1 head of broccoli,
  roughly chopped
1 tbsp olive oil, plus
  extra (optional)
salt and freshly
  ground black
  pepper, to taste

We all know broccoli is good for us, but how do we incorporate it into our diet more imaginatively than just sticking it on the side of the plate? Broccoli mash is the new cauliflower mash. It's so easy to make and has both detoxifying and anti-inflammatory benefits for the body.

Rub the sea bass fillets with salt and pepper and set aside.

Heat a small frying pan to a medium–high heat and toast the walnuts for a few minutes, shaking the pan to prevent them burning, until toasted and browned. Tip onto a plate to cool. Using the same pan, quickly cook the capers for a few minutes then transfer to a plate.

Heat half the oil or butter in a frying pan on a medium heat, then add the onion and cook for 5 minutes. Add the garlic and cook for another minute, stirring well.

Steam the broccoli over a pan of simmering water for 5 minutes until cooked through, then drain off the liquid. Blend the cooked broccoli with the onion mix and a pinch of salt, adding a little olive oil if needed.

Heat the pan in which you cooked the onions with the remaining tablespoon of oil or butter and sear the fish, skin side down, first for 3 minutes until the skin is crisp and then flip it over for another minute until just cooked through.

Mix the toasted walnuts with the capers and olive oil. Spoon the broccoli mash onto two plates, top with the fish and sprinkle over the walnut-caper mix.

bloat-free BLT

serves 4

2 tbsp sunflower
   seeds
8 bacon rashers
2 ripe avocados,
   peeled and stoned
4 leaves of an
   iceberg lettuce
1 beef or heirloom
   tomato, cut into
   1cm slices
salt, to taste

pesto
50g pistachios (or
   pine nuts)
50g fresh mint
   leaves
1 garlic clove
juice of 1 lemon
100ml olive oil

We all love bacon, and when eating healthily it's often hard to find a way to keep it in our diets without dreaming of it between two bits of bread. I think lettuce makes a great alternative to bread, and a couple of large leaves holds together this tasty BLT-with-a-twist with ease.

First make the pesto. Blend the pistachios, mint leaves, garlic and half the lemon juice together in a food processor. Slowly add the olive oil in a constant stream until all the ingredients are combined and you have a smooth pesto.

Heat a small frying pan to a medium–high heat and toast the sunflower seeds for a few minutes, shaking the pan to prevent them burning, until crisp and browned. Tip onto a plate to cool. Using the same pan, fry the bacon until crispy. Slice the avocados and coat them in the remaining lemon juice and add a pinch of salt.

Grab a large lettuce leaf and place in it ½ avocado, 2 rashers of bacon, a dollop of pesto, a few slithers of tomato and some sunflower seeds. Wrap it up, then repeat with the remaining lettuce leaves and ingredients.

beef burger with tomato relish and kale salad

Make sure you buy good-quality grass-fed organic meat to make the best burgers. Rather than reaching for the ketchup, I love serving these with a delicious home-made tomato relish that tastes so much better than the shop-bought stuff.

Heat a small frying pan to a medium–high heat and toast the sesame seeds for a few minutes, shaking the pan to prevent them burning. Tip onto a plate to cool.

Combine the beef mince with the tomato purée, smoked paprika, cumin and a big pinch of salt. Roll the mixture into 4 patties, transfer to a plate, cover and place in the fridge.

Meanwhile, make the relish. Add the tomatoes to a blender with the rest of the relish ingredients. Whizz until combined but still a little chunky.

Mix the honey, olive oil, vinegar, garlic and a pinch of salt together and massage into the kale for a few minutes until it wilts. Throw over the toasted sesame seeds.

Heat a griddle pan and cook the burgers for 3–4 minutes on each side until browned but rare in the middle.

Serve the burgers with a dollop of relish and sauerkraut. Mix the rest of the relish with the kale and serve on the side.

makes 4 burgers for 2

1 tbsp sesame seeds
500g beef mince
2 tbsp tomato purée
2 tsp smoked paprika
1 tsp ground cumin
1 tbsp runny honey
2 tbsp olive oil
1 tsp cider vinegar
1 garlic clove, crushed
50g kale, stems removed, leaves thinly sliced
4 tbsp sauerkraut
salt, to taste

tomato relish
200g beef tomatoes, roughly chopped
1 shallot
4 tbsp chopped fresh coriander
½ tsp cayenne pepper
½ tsp cumin seeds
½ tsp salt
2 tbsp balsamic vinegar

spicy steak with sweetcorn mash

All meat lovers will love this. A big juicy steak, cooked to perfection, is nothing without sweetcorn mash – it's going to be your new favourite! Sweetcorn is a great source of essential minerals and always pairs well with smoky paprika. Serve this to your mates and you'll be friends for ever.

Heat 1 tablespoon of the oil or butter in a pan on a low-medium heat and cook the spring onions and smoked paprika for 3–5 minutes until golden – add a tablespoon of water if it starts to burn. Throw in the corn kernels and half the lime juice and cook for 5 minutes, then remove from the heat and mash the mixture or purée in a blender.

Heat a griddle pan with the remaining oil or butter to a high heat and sear the steaks for 2 minutes on each side until golden on the outside but still rare in the middle. Transfer to a plate to rest, then slice into thin slithers.

Divide the sweetcorn mash among the two plates, and arrange the meat slices over the top. Scatter over the chilli and drizzle over the remaining lime juice and some olive oil. Season with salt and pepper and serve.

serves 2

2 tbsp coconut oil or butter
2 spring onions, finely sliced
½ tsp smoked paprika
3 sweet corncobs, kernels sliced off, or 600g sweetcorn from a can, drained
juice of 1 lime
2 fillet or sirloin grass-fed steaks
1 chipotle chilli, deseeded and finely chopped
olive oil, to serve
salt and freshly ground black pepper, to taste

30 mins

courgette and halloumi mini frittatas with lemon poppy seed yoghurt

Looking for a light lunch? Look no further. Halloumi goes really well with something a little sweet, so this lemon poppy seed yoghurt is the perfect accompaniment.

serves 2

1 tbsp coconut oil
2 eggs
200g halloumi or mozzarella, grated
4 medium courgettes, grated, excess water squeezed out
grated zest and juice of 1 lemon
2 tbsp chopped basil leaves
½ tsp chilli flakes
100g natural yoghurt
1 tsp poppy seeds
1 tsp honey
sea salt and freshly ground black pepper, to taste

Preheat the oven to 200°C/400°F/gas mark 6. Line 4 sections of a muffin tray with baking paper.

Whisk the eggs in a large bowl and mix in the grated cheese, courgettes, lemon zest, chopped basil and chilli flakes. Season with salt and a good grind of pepper. Evenly divide the mix among the 4 greased sections of your muffin tray and cook for 18–20 minutes until golden on top.

While this is cooking, mix the yoghurt, poppy seeds, honey and the juice of half the lemon together.

Serve the frittatas with the poppy seed yoghurt, the remaining lemon juice and sea salt.

10
mins

tuna ceviche with charred lettuce and avocado

serves 2

400g high-grade,
 sashimi-style tuna
 steak, cut into
 2cm cubes
grated zest of
 2 limes, juice
 of 2½ limes
1 tbsp finely grated
 ginger
3 tsp sesame oil
3 tbsp tamari
2 tbsp sesame
 seeds
2 baby gem
 lettuces, cut in
 half lengthways
1 large avocado,
 peeled and stoned
½ tsp freshly
 grated ginger
1 red chilli,
 deseeded and
 finely chopped
2 spring onions,
 finely chopped
salt, to taste

This is seriously sensational in summer. Not only do avocado and tuna go amazingly well together they are also both packed with healthy fats, meaning you'll get a good dose of omega-3 fatty acids and will feel full for longer.

Mix the tuna with the zest and juice of 2 limes, the ginger, 2 teaspoons of the sesame oil and the tamari and leave to marinate while you prepare the rest of the dish.

Heat a small frying pan to a medium–high heat, throw in the sesame seeds and toast them for a minute until golden. Transfer the seeds to a plate to cool.

Heat a griddle pan on a high heat. Brush the lettuce halves with the remaining 1 teaspoon of sesame oil and season with salt. Place the lettuces cut side down on the griddle and cook until crispy, then flip them over and cook for another minute until cooked through.

Mash or blend the avocado with the remaining lime juice, ginger and a pinch of the chilli.

Serve the tuna ceviche with the charred lettuce and a dollop of the avocado cream, then sprinkle over the toasted sesame seeds, remaining chopped chilli and the spring onions.

baked lamb rump with
rosemary cauliflower mash

Swap your weekly steak for lamb with cauliflower mash
– it's bursting with flavour and will leave you feeling
satisfied. You might need to take a trip to the butcher to
get this particular cut of lamb.

Preheat the oven to 190°C/375°F/gas mark 5.

Trim off any excess fat on the lamb and score the top with a sharp
knife. Season with salt and pepper and sprinkle over the rosemary.

Heat a pan with the oil or butter and cook the lamb fat side down
for 4 minutes, turning it over every minute until browned. Pop it in
the oven for 15 minutes then leave to rest for 5 minutes.

To make the cauliflower mash, cook the cauliflower in a pan of
boiling water for 7–10 minutes, until it is cooked through. Drain.

Meanwhile, heat the oil or butter in a frying pan and throw in the
onion. Sauté for 3 minutes then add the garlic, a big pinch of salt
and the rosemary. Cook for another 3 minutes then leave to cool
slightly. Mash the onion mix with the cauliflower, scraping out all the
spices and oil from the pan.

Serve the mash and lamb together with a drizzle of olive oil, salt and
pepper and a pinch of chilli flakes.

serves 2

2 lamb rumps
   (about 250g each)
1 tsp dried
   rosemary
1 tbsp coconut oil
   or butter
olive oil, to serve
chilli flakes, to
   serve
salt and freshly
   ground black
   pepper, to taste

cauliflower mash
1 cauliflower,
   roughly chopped
1 tbsp coconut oil
   or butter
1 onion, finely
   chopped
2 garlic cloves,
   crushed
1 tbsp dried
   rosemary

lamb cutlets with salsa verde

Lamb is such an underrated meat. I love using organic grass-fed lamb for this dish, as it contains more nutrients (not to mention it tastes better). This minty salsa verde will take your lamb cutlets to a whole new level of goodness.

Rub the lamb in the coconut oil, chilli flakes, thyme, cumin, pepper and a big pinch of salt. Leave to marinate while you make the salsa verde.

Place all the salsa verde ingredients in a food processor with a big pinch of salt, blend until smooth, taste, then add more seasoning if needed. Blend again and transfer to a serving pot or glass.

Heat a griddle pan to a medium heat and grill the cutlets for 4–5 minutes each side until golden on the outside and pink in the middle. Serve with a slather of salsa verde and the Mango and Avocado Salad (pages 96–7).

serves 4

8 lamb cutlets
2 tbsp melted
  coconut oil
1 tsp chilli flakes
1 tsp dried thyme
½ tsp ground
  cumin
1 tsp freshly ground
  black pepper
salt, to taste

salsa verde
1 garlic clove
1 shallot
1 tbsp capers
1 tbsp Dijon
  mustard
25g fresh coriander
25g fresh basil
  leaves
handful of fresh
  mint leaves
grated zest and
  juice of 1 lime
150ml olive oil

SLOW

brunch

cinnamon sweet potato bread with caramelised banana

serves 8–10

500g sweet
  potatoes, peeled
  and cut into 5cm
  cubes
110g coconut oil or
  butter
250g coconut sugar
1 vanilla pod, seeds
  scraped
1 egg
4 tbsp almond, rice
  or coconut milk
2 tsp ground
  cinnamon
1 tsp baking
  powder
½ tsp bicarbonate
  of soda
275g buckwheat
  flour
200g walnuts,
  roughly chopped

banana
1 tsp coconut oil or
  butter
½ tsp ground
  cinnamon
1 tbsp honey
1 banana, sliced in
  half lengthways

We often find that the weekend is a time to let loose and relax our diets a bit. However, you don't have to compromise on adventurous breakfasts just because you're on a sugar-free diet. This sweet potato bread contains complex carbohydrates, which means it provides slow-burn energy and you'll feel full until lunch without feeling bloated. Delicious with fresh berries, a dollop of yoghurt and some almond butter.

Preheat the oven to 180°C/350°F/gas mark 4. Line a 900g loaf tin with baking paper, leaving a little hanging over each end.

Steam the sweet potato chunks over a pan of simmering water for 15 minutes or until soft. Leave to cool for a few minutes then purée in a food processor or using a hand-held electric blender. In a clean food processor bowl, or using a hand-held electric mixer, cream the oil or butter and the sugar. Add the vanilla seeds, egg, milk, pureed sweet potato, cinnamon, baking powder, bicarbonate of soda and flour to the food processor and mix well. Fold in the walnuts, crushing them slightly with a wooden spoon. Pour the mixture into the loaf tin and bake for 50 minutes–1 hour or until cooked. Test by poking a skewer into the centre – if it comes out clean, it is done. Remove from the tin and cool on a wire rack.

While the loaf cools, heat the oil or butter in a pan with the cinnamon and honey for 1 minute. Cook the banana halves in the pan for 2–3 minutes on each side until cooked through and golden. Slice the loaf into 2cm-thick slices and serve as it is or toasted, with the caramelised banana.

The loaf will freeze in a freezer bag for a month or will keep in the fridge for a week.

coconut and apricot granola

makes 16 portions

150g coconut oil
1 tbsp vanilla
  extract or
  2 vanilla pods,
  seeds scraped
2 tsp ground
  cinnamon
75g runny honey
250g oats
100g pumpkin
  seeds
100g sesame seeds
100g dried apricots,
  chopped
100g sultanas
100g coconut flakes

This spiced granola tastes like Christmas in a bowl, but it can be enjoyed all year round. Once you've made a batch it is the perfect get-up-and-go breakfast because it can be quickly eaten before you head out of the door to work. Dried fruit and seeds are great because they will keep your energy levels up so you won't be tempted to reach for something sugary mid-morning.

Preheat the oven to 150°C/300°F/gas mark 2.

Melt the coconut oil in a pan set over a low heat with the vanilla, cinnamon and honey. Place the oats, seeds, dried fruit and coconut in a large bowl and pour over the honey mix. Massage the oil into the dried mix with your hands to get it coated all over. Tip the mix onto a 30cm baking tray and bake for 30–35 minutes, stirring it every 10 minutes so it cooks evenly. You want it to be golden and crunchy, but not burnt. Leave to cool on the tray and when cool, transfer to a sealed container. It will keep for 1 week at room temperature.

Serve 40g of the granola with 100ml of almond milk or rice milk and fresh berries.

walnut and raisin fruit loaf with ricotta and berries

A fruit loaf like this is such a great pre-workout snack. The nuts, dates and dried fruit are all high in energy, so a bite or two of this and you'll be able to get the most out of your exercise session.

Preheat the oven to 180°C/350°F/gas mark 4. Line a 1kg loaf tin with baking paper.

Cream the butter and sugar in a food processor, add the egg, dates, vanilla and grated apples and pulse to combine. Sift in the baking powder, bicarbonate of soda and flour with a pinch of salt and the cinnamon. Fold in the walnuts and raisins and process for 5 seconds so the nuts and raisins are mixed in well but not too broken up.

Pour the mixture into the tin, smoothing over the top gently, and bake for 50 minutes–1 hour until just cooked through. To see if the loaf is cooked, insert a skewer in the middle – if it comes out clean, it is done. Leave the loaf to cool in the tin for a few minutes, then transfer to a wire rack to cool completely. Top with sesame seeds.

Cut into inch-thick slices and toast. Serve with ricotta or yoghurt and berries.

makes 1 medium loaf

120g unsalted butter
200g coconut sugar
1 egg, beaten
200g Medjool dates, pitted
1 vanilla pod, seeds scraped
2 apples, grated
1 tsp baking powder
½ tsp bicarbonate of soda
280g rice or buckwheat flour
pinch of salt
1 tsp ground cinnamon
200g walnuts, chopped
75g raisins
1 tbsp sesame seeds
100g ricotta or Greek yoghurt/ coconut yoghurt
200g seasonal berries, such as raspberries or blueberries

fig granola bars

Figs are high in natural sugars, minerals and antioxidant vitamins A, E and K, and because of that beautiful natural sweetness they are the perfect fruit to add to granola. I love keeping a bunch of these bars in the fridge – they are the ideal on-the-go breakfast or snack.

makes 16 bars
200g rolled oats (gluten-free, if you like)
100g sunflower seeds
50g sesame seeds
100g pumpkin seeds
120g runny honey
120g tahini or almond butter
3 tbsp coconut oil
1 tsp vanilla extract
1 tsp ground cinnamon
pinch of salt
1 tbsp freshly grated ginger
200g dried figs, chopped into 1cm slithers
  (or use raisins, if you prefer)

Put the oats, sunflower, sesame and pumpkin seeds in a large pan on a medium heat and cook, stirring, until they have turned golden. Tip onto a plate to cool. Put the honey, tahini or almond butter, oil, vanilla, cinnamon, salt and ginger in a pan (you can use the same pan again) on a gentle heat and cook, stirring, until fully combined.

Tip the cooled oats and seed mix and dried figs into a mixing bowl. Pour over the honey and spices and massage well with your hands so that everything is combined and coated. Line a 20cm x 30cm baking tin with baking paper and spoon in the mixture, smoothing it with the back of a spoon. Cover with cling film and put in the freezer for 1 hour to firm up. Once set, slice into bars and store in a sealed container in the fridge for up to 1 week.

baked apple and blueberry oats with ginger coconut cream

serves 6

2 x 400ml cans
  coconut milk
180g rolled oats
1 tsp baking
  powder
1 tsp ground ginger
 1 tsp ground
  cinnamon
½ tsp vanilla
  extract
3 apples
100g raisins
200g blueberries
2 eggs
9 tbsp honey
2 tbsp coconut oil
150g pecans or
  walnuts, roughly
  chopped
150g pumpkin
  seeds
50g coconut flakes
1 tbsp finely grated
  ginger
salt, to taste

Baked oats are the dream, and this apple and blueberry version is no exception. If you've never tried baked oats, it's a beautiful fluffy porridge that you cook in the oven. Try it – it's a total weekend wonder that will wow your whole family.

Preheat the oven to 180°C/350°F/gas mark 4. Line a 20cm square baking tray with baking paper.

Open the coconut milk cans: there should be a layer of cream at the top and milk at the bottom. Remove the cream from the top of both cans and leave to the side, reserving the milk for the next step.

In a large mixing bowl, combine the oats, baking powder, ginger, cinnamon, vanilla and a pinch of salt. Grate the apples and throw them in with the raisins and blueberries. Stir until well mixed.

Beat the eggs in a separate large bowl, pour in the coconut milk from the cans along with 6 tablespoons of the honey and mix well, then tip in the oat mix, stirring well until evenly mixed. Pour the oat mixture into the baking tray, evenly spreading it out over the base.

In a pan, melt the coconut oil and the remaining 3 tablespoons of honey together with a pinch of salt on a low heat. Throw in the nuts, seeds and coconut flakes and mix well. Pour this on top of the oats mix and place the tray in the oven. Bake for 35–40 minutes until the mixture is golden and crispy on top. Leave to cool while you make the coconut cream.

Heat the reserved coconut cream with the grated ginger, stirring well, for 5 minutes. Serve a scoop of the oats with a drizzle of the ginger coconut cream.

spinach bread

makes 8–10 slices

600g spinach
375g buckwheat
flour
1 tsp salt
2 tsp dried oregano
2 tsp dried thyme
2 tsp baking
powder
¼ tsp bicarbonate
of soda
4 eggs
4 tbsp almond or
rice milk
1½ tbsp apple cider
vinegar
100g coconut oil
150g walnuts,
roughly chopped
sesame seeds and
pumpkin seeds,
for sprinkling
freshly ground
black pepper,
to taste

This is possibly one of my favourite loaves. Its rich green colour makes it very photogenic – especially when topped with eggs. I enjoy this for breakfast or lunch and I sometimes even have it as a snack topped with feta.

Preheat the oven to 160°C/325°F/gas mark 3. Line a 450g loaf tin with baking paper.

Boil the kettle, place the spinach in a colander and pour over the boiling water until the spinach starts to wilt. Leave to drain and cool.

In a large bowl, mix the flour, salt, oregano, thyme, baking powder and bicarbonate of soda together with a good grind of pepper.

In a food processor, blitz the wilted spinach with the eggs, milk, vinegar and coconut oil until smooth but not foamy. Throw in the walnuts and blitz again so they get slightly broken down.

Pour the wet mixture into the dry, stirring well until fully combined. Transfer the mixture to the loaf tin, top it with seeds and bake for 1 hour until cooked through. Leave to cool in the tin, then turn out onto a wire rack to cool completely.

This will keep in the fridge for a week, or you can freeze it for 1 month.

serves 3–4

cannellini bean sausage
2 tbsp avocado oil
4 button mushrooms,
  finely chopped
1 small white onion, finely
  chopped
1 garlic clove
400g can pinto beans,
  rinsed and drained
1 tsp garlic powder
1 tsp fennel seeds
½ tsp salt and freshly
  ground black pepper
1 tsp smoked paprika
½ tsp chilli flakes
½ tsp dried oregano
1 tbsp tomato purée
70g chickpea/gram flour
20g nutritional yeast
1 tbsp tamari
1 tsp xanthan gum

slow-braised beans
1 red onion, cut into ½cm
  chunks
1 carrot, cut into ½cm
  chunks
1 celery stick, cut into ½cm
  chunks
2 garlic cloves, crushed
½ tsp smoked paprika
½ tsp ground cinnamon
2 large beef tomatoes,
  diced
2 tbsp tomato purée
400g can butter beans,
  rinsed and drained
2 roasted red peppers from
  a jar, chopped

sautéed greens
2 garlic cloves, thinly sliced
1 tsp chilli flakes
bunch of Swiss chard, cut
  into 1cm strips
juice of ½ lemon

a vegan full English

Even when we're trying to eat healthily, there's something about a full English that we just crave – especially on the weekend! Whether you're vegan or not, this dish will satisfy that craving and help you get the glow along the way.

Heat 1 tablespoon of avocado oil in a pan on a medium heat and sauté the mushrooms and onion for 5 minutes. Add the garlic and sauté for another minute, then take off the heat to cool.

Boil some water in a pan and place a steamer on top. Put the beans into a large mixing bowl and mash with a fork until broken down but not a pulp. Add the rest of the sausage ingredients and stir well with the fork until everything is fully combined. Divide the mixture into 6 balls and roll each in your hands to make sausage shapes. Grab some tin foil and wrap each sausage separately. Place the foil-wrapped sausages on the steamer, put on the lid and steam for 15 minutes. Remove the sausages from the foil and let them cool on a plate.

To make the braised beans, heat 1 tablespoon of oil or butter in a pan, toss in the onion, carrot and celery and sauté for 5 minutes with a pinch of salt. Throw in the garlic, smoked paprika and cinnamon and stir for 30 seconds. Add the tomatoes, tomato purée, 100ml of water, the butter beans and chopped peppers. Cook for 30 minutes on a low simmer, stirring every 5 minutes. If the mix starts to look dry or is burning on the bottom, add a few tablespoons of water.

About 5 minutes before the sausages and beans are done, heat 1 tablespoon of oil or butter on a medium heat in a large pan, add the garlic and cook, stirring, for 2 minutes, until brown. Throw in the chilli, chard, a big pinch of salt and pepper and cook, stirring well, for 5–6 minutes until the chard is cooked through. Pour in the lemon juice and season if needed.

Heat the remaining tablespoon of avocado oil in a pan and sauté the sausages for a few minutes until slightly golden, then serve with the rest of the dish.

show-stopping *mains* and sides

Malaysian coconut milk laksa with beansprouts and pumpkin

Coconut milk contains mostly medium-chain saturated fatty acids, one of which is lauric acid. Lauric acid is converted in the body to an antiviral and antibacterial compound called monolaurin, which is known to destroy a variety of disease-causing organisms. Want to get rid of that cold? Whip this one up – it's also super comforting when you're feeling run down.

Heat the oil or butter in a pan on a medium heat, throw in the shallots and sauté for a minute, then add the garlic, chilli, coriander and ginger with a pinch of salt. Keep cooking for 5 minutes until the vegetables have softened.

Throw in the pumpkin cubes and cook, stirring well, for a few minutes, adding another pinch of salt, if you like.

Pour in the stock and coconut milk, bring to the boil and then reduce to a low simmer. Cook for 30 minutes with the lid on until the pumpkin is cooked through.

Throw in the mangetout and the beansprouts and cook for a further 3 minutes. Stir in the lime juice and tamari and serve in bowls.

serves 4

1 tbsp coconut oil or butter
6 shallots, finely diced
6 garlic cloves, crushed
1 red chilli, deseeded and finely sliced
1 tbsp ground coriander
2 tbsp freshly grated ginger
1 pumpkin, peeled, deseeded and chopped into cubes
1 litre vegetable stock or chicken stock
400ml can coconut milk
200g mangetout, finely sliced into matchsticks
200g beansprouts
juice of 2 limes
1 tbsp tamari
salt, to taste

roasted sweet potato
with flaked almonds

Sweet potatoes are the perfect side dish to go with any meal, especially when they're roasted. I love serving this with my Whole Apricot-Glazed Chicken (pages 196–7).

Preheat the oven to 180°C/350°F/gas mark 4.

Add the oil or butter to a pan on a low heat with the cumin, chilli, garlic, thyme, lemon zest and juice. Stir everything together until melted and combined. Pour the melted spiced oil into a roasting tin and add the sweet potato wedges, turning them in the oil to coat. Sprinkle over some salt and pop in the oven for 45–50 minutes until the sweet potato is golden and cooked through.

While this is cooking, heat a small frying pan to a medium–high heat and toast the almonds for a few minutes, shaking the pan to prevent them burning, until golden. Tip onto a plate to cool.

Serve the sweet potato with the toasted almonds scattered over.

serves 4

2 tbsp coconut oil
  or butter
1 tsp ground cumin
1 tsp chilli flakes
2 garlic cloves,
  crushed
1 tbsp dried thyme
grated zest and
  juice of 1 lemon
500g sweet
  potatoes, cut
  into wedges
50g flaked almonds
salt, to taste

vegan roast fennel tarts

makes 6 small (12cm) tarts

125g melted coconut oil or butter, plus extra for the tins
2 large fennel bulbs
8 tbsp olive oil
300g rice or buckwheat flour, plus extra for dusting
1 tsp baking powder
200g ground almonds
6 tbsp rice or almond milk
4 spring onions, finely chopped
2 x 400g cans butter beans, rinsed and drained
1 garlic clove
2 tbsp almond butter
2 tsp smoked paprika
2 tbsp apple cider vinegar
salt and freshly ground black pepper, to taste

When my girlfriends come over for dinner in the summer this is my go-to recipe. These tarts are so light and they go down a treat with a big colourful side salad.

Preheat the oven to 180°C/350°F/gas mark 4. Grease six 12cm round tart tins with coconut oil or butter.

Thinly slice the fennel with a mandoline, cover the slices in 2 tablespoons of oil to prevent them browning, and add a big pinch of salt.

Place the flour, baking powder, another big pinch of salt, pepper and the ground almonds in a bowl. Pour over the melted oil or butter and mix it in well, then pour in the milk. Mix everything together well until a pastry forms.

Divide the dough into six balls and roll out each one on a lightly floured work surface to the size of the tart tins. Line the base and sides of the tart tins with the pastry, trimming off any excess. Place the tins on a baking sheet and prick the bottom of the pastry cases with a fork. Transfer the fennel to a roasting tin with the oil and bake alongside the pastry cases for 15–20 minutes until golden. Leave the oven on.

Place the spring onions in a food processor or blender with the butter beans, 6 tablespoons of olive oil, garlic, almond butter, smoked paprika, cider vinegar and a big pinch of salt and pepper. Blend until smooth.

Evenly divide the bean mix between the 6 pastry cases and top with the roasted fennel slithers. Return to the oven at the same temperature and bake for a further 15 minutes until the fennel starts to crisp. Remove from the oven, leave to cool for a few minutes, then dig in.

Once cool, they will keep for a few days in the fridge.

spice up your life
roasted carrots

You can't have a roast without roasted carrots. I love mixing it up a bit from 'easy' steamed or boiled carrots, and cooking them in the oven gives them a nice crisp edge.

serves 4 as a side

500g carrots, cut in half or quarters lengthways
2 tbsp coconut oil or butter
1 tsp ground cumin
¼ tsp cayenne
2 tbsp finely grated ginger
1 lemon
1 tbsp olive oil
salt and freshly ground black pepper, to taste

Preheat the oven to 190°C/375°F/gas mark 5.

Place the carrots in a large roasting tray. Heat the coconut oil or butter in a pan with the cumin and cayenne, ginger and a big pinch of salt and pepper. Pour the spice mix over the carrots and massage it in well. Roast for 45–50 minutes until golden and cooked through.

Serve the carrots with the zest of a quarter of the lemon grated over and the juice of the whole lemon and the olive oil drizzled over.

roast pumpkin, shaved fennel and watercress salad

serves 4 as a side

1kg pumpkin or
  butternut squash,
  peeled, deseeded
  and cut into moon
  shapes
2 red onions,
  peeled and cut
  into quarters
4 garlic cloves,
  roughly crushed
1 tsp dried oregano
½ tsp chilli flakes
3 tbsp melted
  coconut oil
  or butter
2 fennel bulbs
juice of 1 lime
3 tbsp olive oil
1 tsp freshly grated
  ginger
1 tbsp chopped
  fresh mint leaves
  (plus extra leaves
  for serving)
100g watercress
10g fresh coriander
  leaves, finely
  chopped
salt, to taste

Roasted pumpkin or butternut squash is an amazing side dish, whatever the season. Ginger is an incredible natural immune booster, so get this dressing out around autumn time to fire up your body's defences and protect yourself from a cold.

Preheat the oven to 200°C/400°F/gas mark 6.

Place the pumpkin or squash in a roasting tray and nestle the onions and garlic cloves among the pieces. Throw over the oregano, chilli and a big pinch of salt and drizzle over the melted coconut oil or butter, making sure the vegetables are evenly covered. Roast in the oven for 50 minutes until cooked through and golden.

While this is cooking, with a mandoline or sharp knife finely slice the fennel into thin strips, discarding the bottom. Place in a bowl with half the lime juice and 1 tablespoon of the olive oil.

Mix the ginger, mint, remaining 2 tablespoons of olive oil and remaining lime juice in another bowl with a pinch of salt and mix well.

Once the squash is cooked, gently combine with the watercress and fennel, then scatter over the chopped coriander and drizzle over the dressing.

whole apricot-glazed chicken

This is one of my favourite dishes to cook for my family when we catch up with each other on a Sunday night. It's amazing how good a lazy weekend meal with your family can make you feel, especially when it's this good for you!

Preheat the oven to 200°C/400°F/gas mark 6.

Melt 1 tablespoon of oil or butter in a pan, add the shallots and cook for 3 minutes. Chop up 3 of the apricots into small chunks and throw them in with the mustard, vinegar and honey and cook for 5 minutes until the apricots and shallots have softened.

Grab the remaining 5 apricots and cut them in half, then place them on the bottom of the roasting tray and surround them with all the chopped veggies. Rub the chicken all over with the apricot glaze and place it in the middle of the roasting tray on top of the chopped apricots and vegetables. Throw over the thyme leaves and drizzle 2 tablespoons of melted coconut oil or butter over the chicken and veg. Cover in a good pinch of salt and pepper and roast for 1 hour 20 minutes or until the juices run clear when the thigh is pierced with a sharp knife. Remove from the oven and leave to rest for 15 minutes.

Serve topped with freshly chopped basil leaves and dig in.

serves 6

1 tbsp coconut oil or butter, plus 2 tbsp, melted
2 shallots, finely chopped
8 apricots
1 tbsp Dijon mustard
2 tsp apple cider vinegar
2 tbsp runny honey
2 fennel bulbs, cut into quarters
2 parsnips, cut into quarters
3 red onions, cut into quarters
3 carrots, cut into quarters
1.6kg large whole chicken
2 tbsp fresh thyme leaves
2 tbsp freshly chopped basil leaves
salt and freshly ground black pepper, to taste

lamb and spinach curry

I love adding veg to a curry because it gives it a simple vitamin and mineral boost. I've used spinach here as it is great with lamb. Spinach will restore your energy levels, increase vitality and improve the quality of your blood. So next time you make a curry, be sure to drop some in!

Heat the oil or butter in a large pan on a medium heat and throw in the onion. Cook for 4–5 minutes until bronzed and then add the garlic, cayenne, coriander, cumin, turmeric, cinnamon and cardamom. Stir-fry for a few minutes with 4 tablespoons of water until fragrant.

Throw in the lamb with a big pinch of salt and brown for a few minutes – keep adding water if it gets dry so none of the dry spice burns. Pour in the tomatoes, bring the curry to a simmer and cook for 45 minutes, stirring every 15 minutes.

Add the coconut milk – keeping back a few tablespoons to add at the end – stir well and cook for another 45 minutes, stirring every 15 minutes as before. Throw in the spinach and peas and stir again until the spinach wilts. Take the pan off the heat and stir in the lemon juice.

Serve the curry with brown rice, cauliflower rice (pages 122–3) or veg, with a little drizzle of the reserved coconut milk.

serves 4

2 tbsp coconut oil or butter
1 red onion, finely sliced
4 garlic cloves, crushed
1 tsp cayenne
3 tsp ground coriander
3 tsp ground cumin
1 tsp turmeric
½ tsp ground cinnamon
2 cardamom pods
600g lamb shoulder, cut into cubes
2 x 400g cans chopped tomatoes
400ml can coconut milk
200g fresh spinach leaves
200g frozen peas
juice of ½ lemon
salt, to taste

slow-roast beef cheeks with celeriac mash

I lived in France for a little chapter of my life. I'm embarrassed to say that I never picked up much French while I was there but the experience did introduce me to beef cheeks – I used to go into the butcher's shop, puff up my cheeks and the butcher would know what I was cooking for tea!

Heat 1 teaspoon of oil or butter in a frying pan and cook the cheeks with a pinch of salt for a few minutes until bronzed. Tip onto a plate.

Heat the remaining oil or butter in the same pan and fry the onion, celery, thyme and garlic until the veg is softened. Throw this into a slow cooker with the beef cheeks, stock, tomato purée, tomatoes, bay leaf, cinnamon, star anise (if using), a big pinch of salt and some pepper. Heat on a high for 8 hours, stirring every few hours, until the meat falls apart. If you don't have a slow cooker, cook it in a casserole dish with a lid in a preheated oven at a temperature of 140°C/275°F/gas mark 1 for 4–6 hours.

Make the mash 30–40 minutes before the cheeks are ready. Place the celeriac and parsnips in a pot and pour over 400ml of boiling water, then boil the veg for 20–25 minutes until cooked through. Drain, return to the pan and add the 3 tablespoons of oil or butter. Blend until smooth, adding in the cayenne, mustard and the zest of half the lemon.

Serve the mash with the cheeks with some fresh chopped parsley and extra lemon zest scattered over.

serves 6–8

2 tsp coconut oil or butter, plus 3 tbsp for the mash
4 beef cheeks, trimmed of excess fat
2 onions, finely chopped
2 celery stalks, finely chopped
1 tsp dried thyme
3 garlic cloves, crushed
400ml beef or chicken stock
2 tbsp tomato purée
400g can tomatoes
1 bay leaf
1 cinnamon stick
1 star anise (optional)
1 celeriac, peeled and cubed
250g parsnips, peeled and cubed
pinch of cayenne pepper
½ tbsp Dijon mustard
grated zest of 1 lemon
salt and freshly ground black pepper, to taste
fresh chopped parsley, to serve

Moroccan spiced stew with tahini yoghurt

serves 4

1 tbsp coconut oil
  or butter
2 red onions, finely sliced
3 tsp ground cumin
2 tsp ground coriander
2 tsp ground cinnamon
½ tsp cayenne
4 garlic cloves, crushed
½ tsp turmeric
500ml beef or chicken
  stock
400g stewing beef
  or lamb, cut into 2–5cm
  cubes
2 carrots, cut lengthways
  into 5cm chunks
100g green beans
grated zest of 1 lemon
50g toasted pine nuts

spiced tahini yoghurt
3 tbsp tahini
150g Greek yoghurt
juice of ½ lemon
  (2 tbsp)
1 garlic clove, crushed
½ tsp chilli flakes
1 tbsp chopped fresh
  mint leaves, plus extra
  for serving
salt, to taste

There's nothing quite like a warming stew. It's no secret that I have a love affair with my slow cooker – I just love the way it transforms even less-popular cuts of meat into restaurant-worthy meals and this stew is no exception.

Heat the oil or butter in a pan, throw in the onions and cook for 5 minutes. Add the cumin, coriander, cinnamon, cayenne, garlic and turmeric and a few tablespoons of the stock – to prevent the spices burning. Stir well for 30 seconds until fragrant, then add the meat and brown for 30 seconds. Throw in the carrots and pour in the remaining stock, bring to a boil then reduce to a low simmer and cook with the lid on for 1½ hours. After this time, add the green beans and cook for a further 10 minutes.

To make the tahini yoghurt, mix the ingredients together well with a pinch of salt.

Finish off the beef by sprinkling it with the lemon zest and pine nuts and serve with a dollop of tahini yoghurt and some extra fresh mint leaves.

braised beef with crisp tortillas and guacamole

I've never been to Mexico, but it's my dream holiday destination. I love Mexican food and it's so easy to make. These crispy tortillas are a delicious accompaniment – you can whip them up as an alternative to crisps and serve them with homemade guacamole.

Heat the oil or butter in a large pan and sauté the onion for 5 minutes until golden. Add the garlic, chilli, paprika, cumin and a big pinch of salt with a tablespoon of stock so as not to burn the spices and cook for 30 seconds until fragrant. Throw in the meat and cook for a few minutes until browned. Pour in the orange juice and the remaining stock and bring to a boil before reducing to a low simmer. Cook for 2 hours, stirring every 15 minutes until the meat is soft and the juices have almost all been soaked up.

Meanwhile, make the tortillas. Preheat the oven to 180°C/350°F/gas mark 4. In a bowl, mix the flaxseed with 2 tablespoons of warm water and let it sit for 5 minutes. Stir in the chickpea flour, a big pinch of salt, 160ml of water and the cumin and mix until there are no lumps, or blend in a blender until smooth. Heat a small non-stick frying pan with a teaspoon of oil or butter and ladle out 100–125ml of the batter so it just covers the base of the pan. Cook on a medium heat until the edges start to crisp then flip it over and cook until cooked through and it has bronzed marks. Transfer to a plate and repeat with all the batter. Cut the tortillas into quarters and place on a baking sheet. Cook in the oven for 15 minutes, flipping them over halfway through, until they are crisp and golden. Leave to cool.

To make the guacamole, mix the chilli, spring onion and tomato with the garlic, cumin, avocados and lime juice. Mix it all together, keeping it chunky, then stir in a big pinch of salt and the oil. Serve the beef with the guacamole, tortilla chips and some fresh lime juice.

serves 4

2 tbsp coconut oil
  or butter
1 onion, diced
4 garlic cloves, crushed
½ tsp chilli powder
1 tsp smoked paprika
2 tsp ground cumin
500ml beef stock
500g braising beef
juice of 1 orange
salt, to taste

tortilla chips
2 tbsp ground flaxseed
  (flax meal)
90g chickpea flour (gram
  flour)
½ tsp ground cumin
coconut oil or butter, for
  cooking

guacamole
1 red chilli, deseeded and
  finely chopped
1 spring onion, finely
  sliced
1 beef tomato, finely
  sliced
1 garlic clove, crushed
½ tsp ground cumin
2 avocados, peeled,
  stoned and flesh cut
  into chunks
juice of 1 lime, plus extra
  to serve
1 tbsp olive oil

black bean shepherd's pie with parsnip mash and easy peas

serves 4

1 tbsp coconut oil
   or butter
1 onion, finely chopped
2 celery sticks, finely
   chopped
2 garlic cloves, crushed
½ tsp smoked paprika
1 red pepper, deseeded and
   thinly sliced
2 carrots, grated
400g can black beans,
   rinsed and drained
2 tbsp tomato purée
400g can tomatoes
500g parsnips, finely sliced
pinch of ground cinnamon
2 tbsp almond, organic
   cow's or rice milk
1 tbsp coconut oil
   or butter
1½ tsp Dijon mustard
salt and freshly ground
   black pepper, to taste

easy peas
250ml veggie or chicken
   stock
350g peas
2 little gem lettuces, finely
   sliced
grated zest of ½ lemon
2 tbsp toasted hazelnuts,
   chopped

The thing I love about this dish is that all the elements are so great together, but you can also break them down and eat them separately, too. Why not whip up the bean base as a chilli with some avocado, or team some sausages with the mash and peas? Don't get me wrong, this shepherd's pie is a winning combo, but it's extremely versatile, too, so you can really mix it up.

Heat a pan with the oil or butter and sauté the onion and celery for 5 minutes, until softened. Throw in the garlic and smoked paprika and cook for another 30 seconds, then add the pepper and carrots. Cook for another 5–8 minutes until the veg are golden. Add the beans to the mix with the tomato purée and canned tomatoes and cook for 20 minutes on a low simmer – adding a few tablespoons of water at a time so the bean mix doesn't burn.

While this is simmering, preheat the oven to 200°C/400°F/ gas mark 6 and prepare the parsnip mash. Boil the parsnips with a pinch of salt for 10–15 minutes until cooked through. Drain, then return the parsnips to the pan with the cinnamon, a big pinch of salt, a good grind of pepper, the milk, oil and mustard. Blend well or mash until smooth.

Tip the bean mix into a medium ovenproof dish and spoon over the parsnip mash. Bake in the oven for 20 minutes until golden on top and bubbling.

To make the peas, bring the stock to the boil in a large pan. Reduce to a simmer, throw in the peas, lettuce, lemon zest and a big pinch of salt. Cook for 4–5 minutes, drain, then throw over the toasted hazelnuts to serve.

beef brisket with BBQd charred corn

serves 8

beef brisket
1.5kg beef brisket
1 tsp ground cinnamon
2 garlic cloves, minced
500ml beef stock
100g tomato purée
400g can tomatoes
3 tbsp Dijon mustard
3 tbsp tamari
1 tsp smoked paprika
1 fresh chilli, deseeded
  and finely chopped
1 bay leaf
rocket leaves,
  to serve
olive oil, to serve

charred corn
4 tbsp coconut oil or
  butter, melted
grated zest and juice of
  1 lime
1½ tsp smoked paprika
1 jalapeño pepper,
  finely minced
pinch of salt
8 corn on the cobs
small bunch coriander,
  finely chopped

It's no secret that I love slow-cooked meat. The lazy person inside me adores popping this on in the morning and coming home to fall-off-the-bone beef. The charred corn marries so well with the smoked flavour of the meat, plus slow-cooking retains more nutrients because they aren't killed off by high heat.

Rub the beef with the cinnamon and garlic. Place the meat in a large lidded pan and add the stock, tomato purée, tomatoes, mustard, tamari, smoked paprika, chilli and bay leaf. Bring to the boil and let it simmer for 4 hours until the meat is falling off the bone. You can also cook this in a slow cooker – on high for 7–8 hours.

Make the corn about 25 minutes before the beef is done. Mix together the melted oil or butter, lime zest and juice, smoked paprika and jalapeño pepper with a big pinch of salt. Brush the corn with half of the oil or butter blend and wrap each one in a layer of foil. Grill on a preheated barbecue or griddle pan for 5 minutes on each side, rotating 3 times while grilling, then remove the foil and place the corn cobs directly onto the barbecue or griddle pan for another 5 minutes to give them some colour and a smoky flavour.

Remove from the heat and top with chopped coriander and the remaining spiced oil. Serve the beef and corn together with some fresh rocket and olive oil.

thyme-crusted slow-roast pork with poppy seeds slaw

There's nothing better than a big roast, and this slow-roasted pork is perfect for a Sunday night. I've packed this recipe with spices that will be absorbed during slow cooking, which means the end result will be bursting with flavour – a real crowd-pleaser.

Preheat the oven to 220°C/425°F/gas mark 7.

Score the pork fat a little (but don't cut through to the meat), then rub the whole shoulder with the fennel seeds, thyme and lots of salt and pepper. Place in a roasting tin with 250ml of water and roast for 30 minutes. Turn down the heat to 160°C/325°F/gas mark 3, cover the pork in foil and roast for 5 hours, basting the meat with the cooking liquid halfway through. Once the meat is falling off the bone, remove it from the oven and leave to rest, still covered in foil, for 15 minutes.

Mix the vinegar, honey, oil, mustard and dill together. Throw in the fennel, celeriac, poppy seeds and apples with a big pinch of salt and pepper. Mix well and serve with the pork.

serves 6–8

2kg pork shoulder, bone in
2 tbsp fennel seeds
2 tbsp dried thyme
2 tbsp apple cider vinegar
2 tsp runny honey
1 tbsp olive oil
2 tsp Dijon mustard
2 tsp freshly chopped dill
2 fennel bulbs, thinly sliced
1 celeriac, thinly sliced
2 tbsp poppy seeds
3 apples, thinly sliced
salt and freshly ground black pepper, to taste

seafood cauliflower paella

I love paella; it reminds me of a trip to Spain I took with my boyfriend. I'm not too keen on how bloated the rice makes me feel afterwards, though, so I've substituted it with cauliflower grains. You're going to love this – it's a real family recipe that can be enjoyed by everyone!

Heat the stock in a pan to a high simmer, add the saffron then take the pan off the heat and set aside for the flavours to infuse.

Heat the coconut oil or butter in a large pan, throw in the onion, garlic, chorizo and smoked paprika and cook for 5 minutes until golden. Throw in the peppers and saute for 5 minutes. Pour in the tomatoes and chilli flakes, then stir well. Leave this cooking on a low simmer for 5 minutes while you prepare the cauliflower.

Place the cauliflower in the food processor and pulse until it is broken down into rice-like shapes. Add the rice and stock to the tomatoes and cook for 15 minutes on a medium simmer, stirring every few minutes.

Throw the prawns, mussels and monkfish into the paella and cook for 5 minutes. Just before serving, throw in the peas, parsley and lime zest and juice. Serve with a drizzle of olive oil and sea salt.

serves 4

500ml chicken or fish
    stock
2 pinches of saffron
1 tbsp coconut oil or
    butter
1 onion, finely chopped
4 garlic cloves, crushed
100g chorizo
1½ tsp smoked paprika
1 red pepper, deseeded
    and thinly sliced
1 yellow pepper,
    deseeded and thinly
    sliced
400g can chopped
    tomatoes
½ tsp chilli flakes
1 cauliflower, roughly
    chopped
150g king prawns,
    shell on
20 mussels, cleaned
    and debearded
150g monkfish, cut into
    5cm chunks
200g frozen peas
10g flat-leaf parsley,
    finely chopped
grated zest of
    ½ lime, juice of
    1 lime
olive oil, to serve
sea salt, to taste

one-pot chicken and parsnip stew

We often complain that we can't be bothered to cook because the washing-up takes so long. If that's how you feel, this tasty winter dish is for you – it can be cooked in just one pot. Quick and easy to prepare, cooking all the ingredients together means they will retain their delicious flavours.

Preheat the oven to 200°C/400°F/gas mark 6.

Place the chicken in a bowl with the thyme, rosemary, garlic and a big pinch of salt and pepper. Heat 1 tablespoon of oil or butter in a large pan with a lid or a casserole dish, throw in the chicken, brown each piece for a few minutes then transfer it to a plate – you might need to do this in batches for even cooking.

Heat the remaining tablespoon of oil or butter on a medium heat in the same pan, throw in the parsnips and onions and cook for a few minutes until bronzed. Pour over the chicken stock and add a pinch of salt and pepper. Throw in the sage leaves and parsley and stir well. Return the chicken to the pan and stir in the lemon zest and juice. Place in the oven with the lid on and cook for 1 hour.

Remove from the oven and allow to rest for 5 minutes before serving.

serves 6

1kg chicken legs and thighs
2 tbsp fresh thyme, finely chopped
2 tsp fresh rosemary, finely chopped
4 garlic cloves, crushed
2 tbsp coconut oil or butter
3 parsnips, chopped into 5cm cubes
3 red onions, chopped into quarters
500ml chicken stock
4 whole sage leaves
10g fresh parsley, finely chopped
zest and juice of 1 lemon
salt and freshly ground black pepper, to taste

Jamaican BBQ chicken with pineapple carpaccio

serves 6

1 chicken,
  butterflied
  (you can ask
  your butcher
  to do this)
juice of 1 lime
2 tbsp freshly
  chopped basil
1 tbsp olive oil
1 red chilli,
  deseeded and
  finely chopped
½ pineapple, cored
  and thinly sliced

marinade
25g coriander roots
3 fresh red chillies
4 garlic cloves,
  crushed
2 tbsp freshly
  grated ginger
4 spring onions,
  roughly chopped
2 tsp dried thyme
1 tsp ground
  cinnamon
2 tsp allspice
2 tbsp runny honey
grated zest and
  juice of 1 lime
2 tbsp olive oil

I love this combination. The sweetness of pineapple tastes so right with smokey BBQ chicken. I've used fresh herbs here as well as flu-fighting ginger and garlic for a marinade that really packs a punch.

Place the marinade ingredients in a blender and blend until they become a paste. Rub the marinade over the chicken, cover and leave to infuse in the fridge overnight.

The next day, place the chicken on the barbecue and cook for 15 minutes, breast side down, then flip over and cook for 30 minutes – the chicken is cooked when the juices run clear when pierced in the thickest part. Let the chicken rest while you make the pineapple carpaccio.

Combine the lime juice, basil, olive oil and red chilli, to taste, and coat the pineapple slices with this mix. Serve the chicken with the carpaccio on the side.

chicken kebabs with cashew satay

makes 6 skewers, serves 2 or 6 as starter

chicken skewers
3 skinless, boneless
  chicken breasts,
  cut into cubes
2 garlic cloves,
  crushed
1 tbsp freshly
  grated ginger
1 tsp ground cumin
¼ tsp chilli powder
½ tsp smoked
  paprika
grated zest of
  1 lemon
salt and freshly
  ground black
  pepper, to taste
1 tbsp coconut oil,
  for cooking

satay dipping sauce
100g cashew nuts
1 garlic clove
200ml coconut or
  almond milk
1 tsp honey
1 tbsp tamari
1 tbsp freshly
  grated ginger
1 tsp Thai red
  curry paste

We all love a satay sauce. Here I've turned this traditional accompaniment on its head by using cashews instead of peanuts. The end result is just as good but has a creamier taste. These kebabs will get you glowing in no time.

Put the chicken cubes in a bowl and add the garlic, ginger, spices, lemon zest and a big pinch of salt and pepper. Rub the mix all over the chicken with your hands to completely coat, then set aside in the fridge to marinate for a few hours or overnight if possible. (This marinade is best made in advance to get the most flavour out of the meat.)

Heat a small frying pan to a medium–high heat and toast the cashews for a few minutes, shaking the pan to prevent them burning, until golden. Tip out onto a plate and leave to cool. Set aside until you are ready to make the sauce.

When you are ready to cook the chicken, place a griddle pan or normal pan on a medium–high heat. Load the chicken breasts onto skewers and pop a tablespoon of coconut oil in the pan. Sear the skewers for 10 minutes, rotating every minute until cooked through.

While they are cooking, make the dipping sauce. Place the toasted cashews in the blender and blend until broken down, then whiz in the rest of the sauce ingredients for a few minutes until smooth. Transfer to a little serving bowl.

Serve the skewers with the dipping sauce and enjoy!

roasted cauliflower and spiced lentils

serves 2 as main and 4 as side

1 cauliflower, chopped into florets
2½ tbsp coconut oil or butter, for cooking
½ tsp chilli powder
pinch of cayenne
1 tbsp maple syrup or honey
50g pecans or walnuts, roughly chopped
1 red onion, finely chopped
3 garlic cloves, crushed
½ tsp ground turmeric
1 tsp ground cumin
½ tsp ground ginger
400g can lentils, rinsed and drained
2 beef tomatoes, chopped into 2cm cubes
2 tbsp flat-leaf parsley, finely chopped
juice of 1 lemon
olive oil, for drizzling
salt and freshly ground black pepper, to taste
1 tbsp flat-leaf parsley (optional), roughly chopped, to serve

I love the taste of cauliflower when it's roasted. Smoky and sweet, it tastes so good here with peppery lentils. I love making this as a side, and if there's any left just pop it into your lunchbox and take it to work!

Preheat the oven to 220°C/425°F/gas mark 7.

Place the cauliflower on a baking tray. Heat 2 tablespoons of oil or butter in a pan on a low heat, add the chilli powder, cayenne, maple syrup or honey and a big pinch of salt. Pour the spiced oil mixture over the cauliflower and mix well with your hands to evenly coat. Roast for 20 minutes then scatter over the pecans or walnuts and cook for another 10 minutes until the cauliflower is golden brown and cooked through.

Place ½ tablespoon of oil or butter in a pan and throw in the onion, and let this cook for 5 minutes. Add the garlic, turmeric, cumin, a big pinch of salt and the ginger. Stir well, sprinkling a tablespoon of water to prevent it getting too dry. Cook for another 30 seconds then add the lentils and tomatoes, stir well, and cook for a further 10 minutes. Add the parsley, pepper and half the lemon juice and cook for another 5 minutes, then set aside.

Mix the cauliflower and lentils together and serve warm with the remaining fresh lemon juice and olive oil. Garnish with parsley, if you like.

sweet potato, quinoa and orange stew

A flavoursome, versatile dish that can be whipped up at any time of year. Make a double batch for dinner and enjoy it for lunch the next day. It's packed with energy-boosting ingredients to keep you on your A-game.

serves 2

2 sweet potatoes, chopped into 2cm cubes
½ tbsp coconut oil or butter
1 tsp freshly grated ginger
2 garlic cloves, crushed
1 tsp Chinese 5 spice
½ red chilli, deseeded and finely chopped
4 spring onions, finely chopped
grated zest and juice of 1 orange
1 tbsp tamari, plus extra to serve (optional)
1 tbsp honey
100g quinoa
salt, to taste

Place the sweet potatoes in a pan filled with 400ml boiling water with a pinch of salt and boil for 10 minutes. Drain.

Place the oil or butter in a pot, throw in the ginger, garlic, 5 spice and chilli and cook for 1 minute then add the spring onions. Cook, stirring well, for a few minutes.

Mix the orange zest and juice with the tamari and honey in a small pan and cook for a minute or two then add the sweet potato and cook for another 10–12 minutes while you make the quinoa.

Boil the kettle and measure out 300ml of water. Wash the quinoa in a sieve and tip it into a pan with 280ml of the boiling water. Bring to the boil, then cook for 12 minutes until tender. Serve the quinoa with the sweet potato stew and extra tamari, if needed.

desserts

baked strawberry and raspberry tart

Strawberries really take me back to my childhood, when we would go strawberry picking in the summer. We can now get these super berries all year round at the supermarket and they look fantastic on a tart to finish off that perfect showstopping meal!

Preheat the oven to 180°C/350°F/gas mark 4. Grease a 23cm diameter round tart tin with coconut oil.

In food processor, whizz the oats, buckwheat flour, ground almonds and baking powder together. Tip into a bowl and add the coconut oil, then pour in the honey and vanilla and mix together with a spoon. Press the pastry into the tin and bake in the oven for 15–20 minutes until lightly browned and cooked through. Remove from the oven and leave to cool.

Meanwhile, make the filling. Pour the orange juice into a pan and warm it through with the honey. Cook for a few minutes more until reduced – almost all the liquid should have evaporated and the sauce should be thick, not runny. Add the strawberries and raspberries and cook for 5 minutes, then carefully pour onto the pastry base. If there is too much liquid, drain it off first.

To make the topping, mix the ground almonds, baking powder, honey, orange zest, pinch of salt and vanilla together in a bowl with your hands. Sprinkle the topping over the fruit and bake in the oven for 20–25 minutes. Serve with flaked almonds scattered over and a dollop of yoghurt.

serves 8

pastry
3 tbsp coconut oil, plus extra for the tin
70g oats
70g buckwheat flour
150g ground almonds
½ tsp baking powder
3 tbsp runny honey
1 tsp vanilla extract

filling
grated zest and juice of 1 orange
1 tbsp runny honey
400g strawberries, hulled and halved
200g raspberries

topping
250g ground almonds
1 tsp baking powder
6 tbsp runny honey
pinch of salt
1 tsp vanilla extract
2 tbsp flaked almonds and natural yoghurt, to serve

raw key lime
mousse

banoffee
mousse

raw key lime mousse

Key lime pie is a real treat to me – I love how the cream and citrus go together. There's no effort involved in this version and you can honestly tell your friends it's just something you threw together! I've used avocado in this recipe to make the green colour as vibrant as possible.

Toast the nuts in a frying pan until golden, shaking the pan occasionally to make sure they don't burn. Tip onto a plate to cool.

Blend the avocados, lime zest and juice with the honey and coconut oil in a blender until smooth. Transfer the mixture to four individual bowls and top each with the cooled nuts and sprinkle over some cinnamon and raw cacao to finish.

serves 4

50g pecans or
  hazelnuts,
  chopped
2 ripe avocados
grated zest and
  juice of 2 limes
2 tbsp runny honey
1 tbsp coconut oil
pinch of ground
  cinnamon, and
  pinch of raw
  cacao, to serve

banoffee mousse

Banoffee pie is a classic and I love finding new ways to enjoy caramel and banana together. In this version I've created a mousse using cashew nuts, which really complements the banana flavour. Impress your friends with this new take on an old recipe – they'll never know it's healthy!

To make the mousse, place everything in a mini food processor and blend until creamy. Divide among three small ramekins or glasses.

To make the caramel, blend all the ingredients in a mini food processor until smooth. Divide the mixture into three and drizzle the caramel on top of the mousse in the ramekins or glasses. Place them in the freezer for 20 minutes to set, then transfer to the fridge until you are ready to serve.

serves 3

mousse
75g raw cashew nuts
  (soaked in water for
  4 hours)
1 ripe banana
40ml coconut milk
1 tbsp coconut oil
3 Medjool dates, pitted

caramel
100g Medjool dates,
  pitted
4 tbsp almond butter
2 tbsp honey
1 tsp vanilla bean
  powder
pinch of salt
2 tbsp coconut milk

choc chip cookies

It took me several attempts to really perfect this recipe because I wanted these cookies to taste the same as traditional chocolate chip ones. I've finally done it and they taste awesome! A real game changer ... I love dunking these into a glass of coconut milk.

makes 12 cookies

150g unsalted butter
175g coconut sugar
1 egg, beaten
1 tsp vanilla extract
200g rice or buckwheat flour
1 tsp baking powder
pinch of salt
150g good-quality dark or milk chocolate, broken into chunks

Preheat the oven to 160°C/325°F/gas mark 3 and line 2 large baking trays with baking paper.

Cream the butter and sugar in a food processor, then add the egg and vanilla and process again. Sift in the flour, baking powder and a pinch of salt and process until fully combined. Throw the chocolate chunks into the dough and process for 30 seconds so the chunks break down a little and are mixed into the dough.

Roll the dough into walnut-size balls and place on a baking tray about 5cm apart. Bake for 12–14 minutes until golden around the outside, then remove from the oven and leave on the trays to cool and harden.

gluten-free raspberry and pistachio brownies

makes 14–16 brownies

200g coconut oil
  or butter
200g good-quality
  dark chocolate
  (minimum 70%
  cocoa solids)
200g coconut sugar
1½ tsp vanilla
  extract
3 eggs, beaten
200g rice or
  buckwheat flour
pinch of salt
200g raspberries
100g pistachios

Healthy brownies are normally raw or contain hidden beetroot or sweet potatoes. In this recipe I've opted for none of the above, as the health benefits of dark chocolate – including the fact that it contains a good dose of magnesium that helps muscles to relax – make these the perfect post-dinner treat. My brownies are gooey with a little crunch from the nuts – and I'm just putting it out there that these actually taste better than the unhealthy alternative!

Preheat the oven to 160°C/325°F/gas mark 3. Line a 25 x 25cm baking tin with baking paper.

Melt the oil or butter with the chocolate in a pan on a low heat. Remove from the heat and leave to cool slightly.

Beat the sugar, vanilla and eggs together until combined. Once the chocolate has cooled a little, pour it into the egg and sugar mix. Sift in the flour and a pinch of salt, stirring well. Stir in half the raspberries and pistachios.

Pour the mix into the baking tin and scatter over the remaining pistachios and berries, pushing them in slightly so their tops can just be seen. Bake for 25-30 minutes until the brownie is just set – you want the outside to be crispy and the centre gooey. Remove from the oven and leave to cool in the tin. Once cool, slice into squares.

They will last for 1 week in and airtight container in a cupboard.

coconut panna cotta with zesty lemon curd

I love coconut, and its creamy texture makes it so great in desserts. I've managed to create a dairy-free panna cotta here that is easy on the tummy. The lemon curd to serve really wows your taste buds with its tangy, zesty flavour.

Pour a quarter of the coconut milk into a medium saucepan and sprinkle evenly with the gelatine or agar. Let the milk sit for 5–10 minutes to allow the gelatin to soften. Heat the milk and gelatin over a medium heat, stirring constantly, until the gelatin is dissolved and the milk begins to steam. Stir the remaining coconut milk and the honey into the warm milk and whisk until all the ingredients are dissolved.

Remove the pan from the heat, and add the vanilla seeds to the coconut milk. Leave the mixture to cool for 10 minutes.

Divide the coconut milk mixture evenly among 6 glasses or small bowls. Cover each tightly with cling film and refrigerate for about 5 hours, or until cold and set.

To make the lemon curd, place half the sugar or honey, the lemon zest and juice and oil or butter in a pan and bring to almost the boil, then take off the heat, stirring well. In a bowl, whisk the remaining sugar or honey with the eggs until well mixed. Allow it to cool slightly.

Pour the lemon mix over the egg mix and whisk well, then pour it all back into the saucepan. Cook over a medium heat for a few minutes until the mixture thickens, then pour on top of the panna cotta, transfer to the fridge and leave for 3–4 hours to set.

To serve, sprinkle the desiccated coconut on top of the finished dessert.

serves 6

2 x 400ml cans
  coconut milk
1 tbsp gelatine or
  agar powder
100g runny honey
2 vanilla pods,
  seeds scraped

lemon curd
125g honey or
  coconut sugar
grated zest and
  juice of 1 lemon
75g coconut oil
  or butter
2 eggs
1 tbsp desiccated
  coconut

coconut macaroons with chocolate dipping sauce

makes 18

4 egg whites
¼ tsp cream of
 tartar
120g coconut sugar
2 tsp ground
 almonds
1 tsp vanilla extract
200g desiccated
 coconut

dipping chocolate
90g cacao butter or
 coconut oil
60g raw cacao
 powder
60g honey or
 maple syrup
pinch of sea salt (or
 Himalayan)

Coconut macaroons and chocolate are a match made in heaven. These are the perfect on-the-go snack and I love popping a few in my bag for that 4 p.m. 'tea and cake break' with a twist.

Preheat the oven to 180°C/350°F/gas mark 4. Line a baking tray with baking paper.

Beat the egg whites until frothy, then add the cream of tartar and whisk until soft peaks form. Slowly mix in the coconut sugar until fully combined, then gently fold in the almonds, vanilla and desiccated coconut.

Grab a tablespoon of the mix, form it into a ball and set it on the baking tray. Repeat until you have 18 balls, then bake them in the oven for 10–12 minutes until golden. Take them out and let them cool and harden on the tray while you make the chocolate sauce.

Melt the cacao butter or coconut oil in a pan on a low heat and slowly sift in the cacao powder, then stir in the honey or maple syrup and salt until everything is combined.

Once the balls and chocolate have cooled spoon 1 tablespoon of chocolate over each coconut macaroon. Place the balls in the fridge to cool so that the chocolate hardens.

These will keep for 4 days in the fridge.

raw ginger crunch

This is such a taste of my childhood. My mum always used to make this and to me it has such a warming and homely taste. I was determined to make a refined-sugar-free version of this for you to enjoy. It's full of dates, so as well as a dessert it makes a surprisingly tasty pre-workout snack, as it will increase your energy levels.

makes 10 pieces

bottom layer
175g dates, pitted
100g cashews
50g desiccated coconut
1 tsp ground ginger
pinch of salt

ginger layer
4 tbsp coconut oil
3 tbsp honey
3 tsp ground ginger

Line a 900g loaf tin with baking paper. To make the base, blend the dates, cashews, desiccated coconut and ground ginger together with a pinch of salt in a food processor. Transfer the mix to the tin.

Place a small pan on a very low heat and add the coconut oil, honey and ginger and stir until melted. Take the pan off the heat and stir until the mixture has cooled and thickened. Pour over the base and place in the fridge for an hour. Once set, cut into 10 squares and store in the fridge.

These will keep for a week.

raw toffee chocolate sticks

These taste as good as they sound. Chocolate lovers take caution, these sticks are pretty addictive! Serve them up for dessert to your friends, they'll be amazed that the caramel is raw and totally refined-sugar-free.

makes 10 pieces

320g Medjool dates, pitted
3 tbsp smooth almond butter
1 tsp fresh lemon juice
¼ tsp fine sea salt
1 vanilla bean, deseeded, or ½ tsp pure ground vanilla bean powder
50g good-quality chocolate (minimum 70% cocoa solids)

Combine the dates, almond butter, lemon juice, salt and vanilla in a food processor until smooth. Spread the mix into a rectangle to a depth of 1cm on a baking tray lined with baking paper. Transfer the tray to the freezer for 2 hours.

Once hardened, cut the toffee mixture into 10 thin 1cm matchsticks. Return to the freezer while you prepare the chocolate.

Melt the chocolate in a pan on a low heat, then take off the heat and leave to cool and thicken. Grab a toffee stick and dunk it into the chocolate, then place it on a plate; repeat with the rest of the mix. Place the sticks in the fridge for 20 minutes for the chocolate to set, then enjoy!

These will keep for 2 weeks in the fridge.

carrot cake muffins

makes 12 muffins

250g coconut oil or
  butter
250g coconut sugar
3 eggs
grated zest of
  1 orange
250g rice flour
1 tsp ground cinnamon
½ tsp ground ginger
2 tsp baking powder
½ tsp bicarbonate of
  soda
250g carrots, grated
150g walnuts, roughly
  chopped

Carrot cake is the ultimate British teatime treat. There's something so irresistible about the taste of carrot cake – the crunchy nuts with sweet carrot and cinnamon are so comforting. Here I'm using coconut sugar, one of my cupboard staples, to sweeten the cakes so you can still have your cake and eat it – the healthy way!

Preheat the oven to 160°C/325°F/gas mark 3. Line the holes of the muffin tray with baking paper.

Cream the oil or butter and sugar in the food processor, then throw in the eggs and pulse. Add the orange zest, flour, cinnamon, ginger, baking powder and bicarbonate of soda and mix well. Stir in the carrots and 100g of the walnuts, stirring well. Divide the mixture among the holes in the muffin tray and top each with the rest of the walnuts. Bake in the oven for 35–40 minutes until just cooked through. Let them cool and dig in.

These will keep in an airtight container at room temperature for 2–3 days.

heavenly hidden cake

This delicious spiced cake tastes exactly as its name suggests: heavenly. The vegetables make this light and moist while providing extra nutrients. The best part? You'd never know there's any veg in it!

serves 8–10

60g coconut oil or butter, plus extra for greasing
1 tsp vanilla extract
3 eggs
90g runny honey
375g ground almonds
1 tsp ground cinnamon
100g carrots, grated
150g apples, grated
150g courgette, grated

Preheat the oven to 180°C/350°F/gas mark 4. Grease a 22cm round cake tin with coconut oil or butter.

In a food processor, blitz the oil or butter with the vanilla, eggs and honey for a minute until smooth, then stir in the almonds with the cinnamon and the grated carrot, apple and courgettes.

Pour the cake mix into the cake tin and bake in the oven for 40–45 minutes or until a toothpick inserted into the centre comes out clean. Leave to cool in the tin, then transfer to a wire rack to cool completely, then dig in!

This cake will keep in an airtight container for 3 days.

meal

plans

get glowing meal plan

	saturday	sunday	monday
breakfast	Baked Apple and Blueberry Oats with Ginger Coconut Cream (page 178)	A Vegan Full English (page 182)	Carrot Bircher (page 50)
lunch	Seafood Cauliflower Paella (page 213)	Moroccan Spiced Stew with Tahini Yoghurt (page 202)	Malaysian Coconut Milk Laksa with Beansprouts a Pumpkin (page 187)
snack	Raw Mango and Coconut Bites (page 104)	Turmeric-tastic (page 38)	Turmeric-tastic (page 38)
dinner	Moroccan Spiced Stew with Tahini Yoghurt (page 202)	Malaysian Coconut Milk Laksa with Beansprouts and Pumpkin (page 187)	Pan-Fried Sea Bass with Spicy Butter Bean Stew (page 138)
next-day prepping	Hop to the shops and get the ingredients for the next few days of recipes. Make a batch of Raw Mango and Coconut Bites (page 104) and enjoy one each day as your snack for the week	Make the Malaysian Coconut Milk Laska (page 187); enjoy for dinner and have the leftovers prepped in your Tupperware for lunch the next day. Whip up a double portion of Turmeric-tastic juice (page 38) for your snack today and tomorrow, and a batch of the Carrot Bircher (page 50). Leave this to soak overnight in the fridge ready for the morning	Place your leftover sea ba in your Tupperware. Get together all your ingredie for breakfast tomorrow

tuesday	wednesday	thursday	friday
Smoked Salmon, Poached Eggs, Chilli-Spiced Yoghurt and Crispy Kale (page 58)	Pimping Porridge with Pomegranate, Poached Pears and Pistachios (page 66)	Avocado on Toast with Tomato, Feta and Mint (page 64)	Coconut and Lime Quinoa Porridge with Honey Almond Crumble (page 57)
Pan-Fried Sea Bass with Spicy Butter Bean Stew (page 138)	Bloat-Free BLT (page 152)	Turmeric Chicken Burgers with Shaved Courgette and Chilli Salad (page 125)	Chickpea and Hazelnut Falafel with Tomato and Pomegranate Salad (page 120)
Raw Mango and Coconut Bites (page 104)	Raw Mango and Coconut Bites (page 104)	Raw Mango and Coconut Bites (page 104)	Raw Mango and Coconut Bites (page 104)
Bloat-Free BLT (page 152)	Turmeric Chicken Burgers with Shaved Courgette and Chilli Salad (page 125)	Chickpea and Hazelnut Falafel with Tomato and Pomegranate Salad (page 120)	Seafood Cauliflower Paella (page 213)
Soak your oats for tomorrow's brekkie. Pop your BLT in your lunchbox	Shop for the next three days. Place leftover chicken burgers in your Tupperware for lunch tomorrow	Soak your oats for Friday's porridge	It's Friday! No need to food prep – you have the weekend to shop, chill, eat and enjoy!

vegetarian meal plan

	saturday	sunday	monday
breakfast	Baked Apple and Blueberry Oats with Ginger Coconut Cream (page 178)	A Vegan Full English (page 182)	Pea Fritters with Smashed Avocado and Poached Eg (page 53)
lunch	Vegan Roast Fennel Tarts (page 190)	Roasted Cauliflower and Spiced Lentils (page 220)	Malaysian Coconut Milk Laksa with Beansprouts ar Pumpkin (page 187)
snack	Butter Bean and Almond Dip (page 102)	Butter Bean and Almond Dip (page 102)	Butter Bean and Almond (page 102)
dinner	Roasted Cauliflower and Spiced Lentils (page 220)	Malaysian Coconut Milk Laksa with Beansprouts and Pumpkin (page 187)	Grilled Halloumi and Man Slaw with Coconut Tahini Dressing (page 88)
next-day prepping	Hop to the shops and get the ingredients for the next few days of recipes. Whip up my Butter Bean and Almond Dip (page 102) and chop up some crudités to go with it to enjoy as snacks for the next few days	Make your pea fritters so they are ready to heat up tommorow for breakfast (page 53) and whip up a batch of Fig Granola Bars (page 177) for your snack for the week ahead. Make the Malaysian Coconut Milk Laska with Beansprouts and Pumpkin (page 187); enjoy for dinner and then have the leftovers prepped in your Tupperware for lunch the next day	Prep two portions of the Pimping Porridge (page 66) ready for breakfast on Tuesday and Wednesday. Pop the halloumi salad int your lunchbox

tuesday	wednesday	thursday	friday
Pimping Porridge with Pomegranate, Poached Pears and Pistachios (page 66)	Pimping Porridge with Pomegranate, Poached Pears and Pistachios (page 66)	Avocado on Toast with Tomato, Feta and Mint (page 64)	Coconut and Lime Quinoa Porridge with Honey Almond Crumble (page 57)
Grilled Halloumi and Mango Slaw with Coconut Tahini Dressing (page 88)	Chickpea Curry (page 118)	Aubergine Stew with Cauliflower Rice (page 123)	Chickpea and Hazelnut Falafel with Tomato and Pomegranate Salad (page 120)
Fig Granola Bars (page 177)	Fig Granola Bars (page 177)	Fig Granola Bars (page 177)	Fig Granola Bars (page 177)
Chickpea Curry (page 118)	Aubergine Stew with Cauliflower Rice (page 123)	Chickpea and Hazelnut Falafel with Tomato and Pomegranate Salad (page 120)	Vegan Roast Fennel Tarts (page 190)
Pack the leftover curry for tomorrow's lunch, and cut up a carrot for crudités to team with the dish	Pop a portion of Aubergine Stew into a container for tomorrow's lunch	Soak your oats for Friday's breakfast feast. Pack your chickpea falafel into your lunchbox and smile – it's the end of the week!	It's Friday! No need to food prep – you have the weekend to shop, chill, eat and enjoy!

yoga

Life is better with yoga: it reduces stress, energises your body and just makes you feel good.

I know it can be tempting to skip exercise when you're pushed for time – I'm guilty of that too – but this easy yoga sequence totally sets me up for the day. I do it every morning and it gets me off on the right foot.

Start your day with a big glass of warm water with 1 tablespoon of freshly grated ginger and 1 teaspoon of turmeric in it. Drink it up, then hop on your mat to begin this quick and energising sequence.

1. savasana

Start by lying on your back, palms facing up, legs hip width apart. Close your eyes and start to tune into your breath. Place your hand on your belly, feeling it rise and fall five times. Try to lengthen your exhale on each breath.

2. pawanmuktasana

This pose is great for digestion relief.

Hug your right knee to your chest, interlock your fingers around your right shin bone and pull the knee as close as you can towards your chest. As you inhale, lengthen the left leg; as you exhale, pull in the right knee a little more. Continue for three more breaths then repeat on the left side.

3. rock and roll

Hug both knees into your chest and start rocking and rolling up and down your spine. Repeat three times until you get enough height to place your hands on the floor.

This pose massages your spine.

4. tabletop

On all fours, push onto your hands and place your legs back into tabletop position. Make sure your knees are below your hips and that your wrists, elbows and shoulders are in line and perpendicular to the floor. Centre your head in a neutral position and look downwards.

5. cow pose

Inhale and peel your sitting bone and chest towards the ceiling while sinking your belly to the floor, eyes looking forward.

This mobilises your spine.

6. cat pose

As you exhale, round your spine towards the ceiling, keeping your shoulders and knees in position, and release your beautiful head towards the floor. Inhale. Repeat Cat and Cow Pose three times to a slow, soft breath, then come back to neutral tabletop.

7. bent knee downward dog

Bring your hands slightly in front of your shoulders, spread your palms, index finger facing forward, and tuck in your toes. On your next exhalation, push up into downward dog with bent knees. Lengthen your tailbone, lifting it towards the ceiling; feel the length through your spine. Walk your legs out, opening up your hamstrings, then come to stillness, working on straightening your legs while keeping a long, straight spine. Inhale for four counts, exhale for four counts. Repeat three times.

8. rag doll

Look towards your hands. Step your feet hip-width apart towards the front of the mat and bend forward over your legs, grabbing your elbows. Sway from side to side. Drop your head, relax your jaw and close your eyes. Breathe into the back of your ribcage, feeling it expand.

9. upward salute

Bend your knees and stretch your arms all the way up above your head and come up, lifting your heart and expanding your chest. Keep your gaze up, and your face relaxed.

10. half-standing forward bend

Exhale and fold forwards; inhale and lift your chin and chest, gazing at the ground in front of your feet. Press your hands into your shins or towards the floor and work on straightening your legs. Exhale and fold forwards once more.

11. plank pose

Exhale. Step back into downward dog, then inhale and draw your torso forward until your shoulders are over your wrists and torso, parallel to the floor. Soften your shoulder blades against your back, round down through your hands and spread your collarbone. Pull your belly in, lift your skull away from your neck and look straight at the floor, face and jaw relaxed. Breathe in and out for four counts, three times.

12. crescent lunge

Inhale, push back to Downward Dog below. Exhale, step your left foot between your hands, aligning your knee over your heel. Inhale and raise your torso upright, sweeping your arms up, palms facing each other. Lengthen your tailbone and reach back through your right heel standing in Crescent Lunge. Stay static and breathe deeply for three breaths, grounding through your feet and reaching through your arms.

13. downward dog

On your next exhalation, cartwheel your hands to the floor, come into Plank position then Downward Dog. Take a breath, then repeat on the other side. Then step to the front of the mat.

14. chair pose

Inhale and raise your arms perpendicular to the floor, palms facing inwards. Exhale and bend your knees, lowering your thighs parallel to the floor. Bring your shoulder blades back, and tailbone towards the floor, keeping your back long and strong. Stay for five slow breaths.

This is a burner but strengthens your thighs and stretches out your shoulders.

15. rock and roll to chair

Rock and roll up and down your spine then push up into Chair Pose above again. Repeat this three times. You can use your hands to help you up, but as you get stronger, use your core to rock you back up to standing.

16. chair pose

Hold chair pose again, inhaling in and exhaling out for three breaths.

17. tree pose

Inhale, reach your arms up over your head, lengthening your body. Bring your arms down and come into a standing pose. Shifting your weight to your left foot, bend your right knee, and with your right hand clasp your right ankle. Place the sole of your foot against your inner left thigh or calf. Centre your pelvis over your left foot, hand on hip, making sure your pelvis is neutral and facing forward. Lengthen your tailbone towards the floor, press your right sole into your inner thigh, press your hands together in prayer, then reach up above you, gaze in front and breathe for five counts. Repeat on the other side.

18. core activation

Exhale, coming back to standing. Inhale, look up, keeping your back flat. Exhale, step back to Plank. Inhale, bring your right knee to your right elbow and hold; inhale, exhale then repeat on the other side. Repeat this sequence three times, engaging your core. Come back to Plank, inhale and exhale once before placing your knees on the floor. To the count of five, lower your belly to the floor keeping your elbows tucked in.

19. sphinx pose

Tuck your tailbone towards your pelvis; lengthen your heels, reaching through your toes, legs active. Set your elbows under your shoulders with your forearms parallel to the floor. Inhale, lift your upper torso and head away from the floor, opening out your chest. Inhale and exhale softly five times. Tuck your toes under and push back so you're sitting on your heels in Child's Pose. Push back into Downward Dog.

20. pigeon pose

Inhale, sweep your right leg up behind you to three-leg dog, then exhale, bringing the right knee to your right wrist, squaring your hips forward. Place your fingertips to the floor; keep your spine long. Inhale; if it feels comfortable, start lowering your torso to the floor, keeping your core engaged. Hold, breathing into your hips for five long breaths. Push back into Downward Dog and repeat on the other side. Come back to Downward Dog, look between your hands, step forward and roll onto your back.

21. bridge pose

Bend your knees and set your feet hip width apart, close to your sitting bones. Inhale and on your next exhalation mindfully roll your tailbone towards the sky, bringing your lower back off the floor, then the middle through to your upper back, keeping your shoulders on the floor. Lift your bottom, keeping your knees directly over the heels, pushing into the feet, and lengthen your tailbone. Slowly roll back down then repeat three times. Rock your knees from side to side before hugging them to your chest.

22. reclining twist

Return to lying on your back. Hug your left knee to your chest and stretch out your right leg. Holding your left knee with your right hand, bring your left knee towards your right, stretching out your left arm to the side and look over to your left palm. Hold for three soft breaths. Repeat on the other side. Hug your knees to your chest.

Twists are great for digestion.

23. savasana

Lying on your back, with your hand lift the base of your skull away from your back and neck, lengthening your neck. With your feet mat-width apart, shoulders soft, palms facing up, close your eyes and breathe softly, from your belly. Watch your breath slow down, feeling it flow inside and out. Repeat this mantra in your head: on your inhalation, think 'let'; on your exhalation, think 'go'. Repeat for a few minutes. Then hug your knees to your chest and roll to your right side.

24. hero pose

Either sit on your heels or in a comfy crossed-legs position. Inhale and bring your hands into prayer in front of your heart. Close your eyes and repeat to yourself silently, 'I am strong, I am healthy, I am happy'.

Open your eyes and have the most awesome day ever!

Remember to hydrate.

After your yoga routine, hop in the shower, whip up your brekkie and head out the door. My favourite post-yoga treat is my Mango Lassi Smoothie (pages 44–5) or my Pimping Porridge with Pomegranate, Poached Pears and Pistachios (pages 66–7).

1

2

7

8

4   5   6

10   11   12

13

14

19

20

16   17   18

22   23   24

index

Page numbers in *italic* refer to the illustrations

acknowledgements

Thank you to Lucy, my right-hand woman, who has been my rock and chief recipe taster.

Thank you to my gorgeous manager, Alice, who has become like a sister to me.

Thank you to my wonderful editor, Anna: you bring such joy and vibrancy to everything you do and made writing this book a joy.

Thank you to everyone at Orion, the best people in publishing. Thank you for your enthusiasm and kindness.

Thank you to Martin, Ellis, Bianca and Olivia for making the food look so delicious and for making me glow.

Thank you to my amazing family, who are so unbelievably supportive and caring.

Thank you to my incredible boyfriend, who I love more than anything.

Thank YOU so much for buying this book. I truly appreciate it and hope you enjoy it.

This edition first published in Great Britain in 2016 by Orion, an imprint of the Orion Publishing Group Ltd, Carmelite House, 50 Victoria Embankment, London EC4Y 0DZ
An Hachette UK Company

10 9 8 7 6 5 4 3 2 1

A CIP catalogue record for this book is available from the British Library.

ISBN: 978 1 4091 6338 1

Photography: Martin Poole, Ellis Parrinder
Food styling: Bianca Nice
Prop styling: Olivia Wardle

Printed in Italy

MIX
Paper from responsible sources
FSC® C023419

Every effort has been made to fulfill requirements with regard to reproducing copyright material. The author and publisher will be glad to rectify any omissions at the earliest opportunity.

www.orionbooks.co.uk

by BOOK or by COOK
COOKING EATING SHARING

For more delicious recipes, features, videos and exclusives from Orion's cookery writers, and to sign up for our 'Recipe of the Week' email visit **bybookorbycook.co.uk**

Follow us

 @bybookorcook

 @bybookorbycook

Find us

 facebook.com/bybookorbycook